Walking as He Walked

Walking as He Walked
with Study Guide

Joel R. Beeke

Reformation Heritage Books
and
Bryntirion Press

Copyright © 2007 Joel R. Beeke

Published by

Reformation Heritage Books
2965 Leonard St., NE
Grand Rapids, MI 49525
USA
616-977-0599 / Fax 616-285-3246
e-mail: orders@heritagebooks.org
website: www.heritagebooks.org

and

Bryntirion Press
Bridgend
CF31 4DX
Wales, UK

ISBN #978-1-60178-010-2

Contents

Preface

When Spurgeon preached his first message in the newly built Metropolitan Tabernacle in March 1861, he made it very clear what he intended to be the major theme of his ministry. His text was Acts 5:42, "And daily in the temple, and in every house, they ceased not to teach and preach Jesus Christ." He lamented the fact that from this message the post-apostolic church soon began a long decline and spoke of ceremonial and church offices rather than the person of our Lord. In our age, Spurgeon affirmed, we too have gone from preaching Christ to preaching doctrines about Christ, inferences which may be drawn from His life, or definitions which may be gathered from His discourses.

Christianity is the Christ of biblical and historical facts. It is a religion of a book authored by men who knew our Savior intimately and were given His inspiration and authority to write about Him. We pass on to our generation and to every single congregation the message they have given to us as the foundation for our lives and the life of our congregations. Paul is our pattern for preaching. He tells the essential

facts about Christ, interprets those facts clearly, and
then urges men to apply the truth by faith to their
lives. The marks of a true ambassador of Christ are
telling and interpreting the life, death, and resurrection of Christ and then pleading with sinners in
Christ's stead to be reconciled to God by repenting
and receiving Jesus Christ as Lord and Savior.

In Aberystwyth, on the west coast of Wales in the
summer of 2006, one such ambassador from Grand
Rapids came once again to our Principality and
delivered four addresses on the example of Christ.
The impact in print is considerable now. To have
heard them delivered "in the wisdom and power of
the Holy Spirit" is even now unforgettable. Dr. Beeke
is in a class of his own when it comes to exegetical
and expository preaching. He never disappoints.
He is always fresh, illuminating, and instructive.
Furthermore, he is not content to be limited by the
immediate text but invariably applies it to the wider
canvas of Holy Scripture and the range of people
listening, converted and unconverted, backsliding
Christian and earnest disciple, those who lack assurance and those who know whom they have believed.
The result is often a mini-theology on such topics as
the person and work of Christ, repentance and faith,
marks of spurious faith, the substitutionary character
of the cross, and the true message of the gospel. The
challenge, application, and constant call for closure
with Christ, marks the whole work. The sermons are

not only didactic, they are thoroughly evangelistic in the biblical sense.

If you believe, as this writer does, that the most urgent need today is for a new reformation and true revival, then what can be said of this book is that it breathes the atmosphere of the Holy Spirit. Naturally, the style is sermonic rather than an academic thesis. But it is so easy to read, immediately impacting, spiritually uplifting, and results in sheer joy and pleasure. Christians of all shades and interests can only be enriched by such material. Young and older will find help here.

—Geoff Thomas

Jesus' Crossbearing and Ours

The theme "Walking as He Walked" is drawn from 1 John 2:6, which says that those who abide in Christ should "walk, even as he walked." John says that if we truly belong to Christ, our manner of life will conform with Christ's. If we are not in Christ, we have not yet begun to walk like Christ; but if we are in Christ, we have begun to walk like Christ. In other words, walking as Christ walked is not optional for the Christian; it is what it means to be a Christian. If we are true Christians, we are striving for more Christlikeness and welcome any help along the way.

We will not, of course, fully reach our goal of Christlikeness until we reach heaven. As the Puritan William Fenner pointed out: "None of us in this life will walk so purely, so unspottedly, so steadily, so effectually as Christ lived, though this is our goal while running the Christian race" (*Works,* p. 315). Just as an aspiring student of art learns from an experienced artist how to paint, so we learn from the perfect Savior how to walk like Him.

Walking as Christ walked is an inexhaustible theme that encompasses all of the Christian life. There are scores of ways in which Christ calls us to walk, think, speak, and live as He did. Walking as Christ walked means making Jesus' priorities my own by faith (John 6:38). It means delighting in and keeping God's law as Jesus did (Ps. 40:8). It means having compassion for others, repaying evil with good, and acting in love (John 13:15; 1 Pet. 2:23; Luke 23:34). It means despising the same pleasures and vanities of this world that He despised, speaking and living the same truths that He spoke and lived, and being led by the same Spirit that led Him (Rom. 8:14).

When I began outlining my first draft of possible ways to address this vast subject, I soon had a list of a dozen or more titles, such as "Jesus' Mind and Our Mind," "Jesus' Peace and Our Peacemaking," "Jesus' Love and Our Love," "Jesus' Mercy and Our Mercy," "Jesus' Servanthood and Our Servanthood," "Jesus' Intercession and Our Praying," "Jesus' Persecution and Our Persecution," and "Jesus' Obedience and Our Obedience." Then, too, I thought about individual chapters that focus on the theme of walking like Christ, such as Ephesians 5, which speaks about walking in Christlike love (v. 2), Christlike light (v. 8), Christlike circumspection (v. 17), and Christlike submission (v. 21). And I thought it would be good to write at least one chapter on how we are *not* to walk like Christ—for we are not to act as if we are divine or partake of Christ's incommunicable attributes. In the end, however, I settled on four ways—all resisted by our natural flesh—in which we must strive to be like Christ: (1) crossbearing, (2) office-bearing, (3) tears, and (4) endurance. Becoming like Christ in each of these ways is challenging; yet, if we learn them from Christ, our Christian walk will greatly profit.

The first subject, then, is crossbearing. Certainly there are few subjects more challenging and more avoided than crossbearing. Yet crossbearing is foundational to our Christian walk. Without bearing your crosses after Christ, you cannot be a Christian. Jesus said plainly in Luke 14:27, "Whosoever doth not bear his cross, and come after me, cannot be my disciple."

In Christian discipleship, the cross or crossbearing is a metaphor for suffering and burdenbearing, and involves the taxing and tasting of the strength of our faith. John Calvin taught that crossbearing is an intimate part of the Christian life. He said that those who are in fellowship with Christ must prepare for suffering. One major reason for this is the believer's perpetual union with Christ. Because Jesus' life was a perpetual cross, ours must also include suffering. Through crossbearing, we not only participate in the benefits of Christ's atonement, but we also experience the Spirit's work of transforming us into the image of Christ.

Crossbearing tests our faith. Through crossbearing, Calvin said, we are roused to hope, trained in patience, instructed in obedience, and chastened for our pride. Crossbearing is our medicine and our chastisement. Through it, we are shown the feebleness of our flesh and are taught to suffer for the sake of righteousness (*Institutes*, 3.8.1-9). For all these reasons, crossbearing is critical for us. How do we learn to do it?

Let's look at the theme of "Jesus' Crossbearing and Ours" by considering how Jesus and Simon the Cyrenian carried the cross. Our texts are Mark 15:21, "And they compel one Simon a Cyrenian, who passed by, coming out of the country, the father of Alexander and Rufus, to bear his cross," and its parallel passage, Luke 23:26, "And as they led him away, they laid hold upon one Simon, a Cyrenian, coming out of the country, and on him they laid the cross, that he might bear it after Jesus." Drawing from these texts, we'll discuss, first, a cursed crossbearer; next, a coerced crossbearer; then, finally, a conquered crossbearer.

A Cursed Crossbearer

Mark 15 shows us how Jesus' own people rejected Him, crying out, "Away with this man; crucify him." They preferred to release from prison Barabbas, a leading criminal, rather than Jesus.

The verses preceding our text detail how Jesus was cruelly mistreated in Pilate's judgment hall. Soldiers placed a crown of thorns on Jesus' head. They slapped His head with a reed, spat upon Him, and mocked Him by robing Him like a king. Then they tore the robe off His bloody back, put His clothes back on, and laid a heavy cross across His shoulders. Jesus was led out of Jerusalem, the city in which God dwelled in the midst of His people. The everlasting Son of God, the only worthy one in Jerusalem, was led out of Jerusalem as an outcast.

Jesus predicted this treatment when He told the parable of the vineyard. In Matthew 21:39, Jesus said, "And they caught him (that is, the son of the master), and cast him out of the vineyard, and slew him." Being cast out of the vineyard is symbolic of those who were carried outside the city after being condemned for a crime worthy of death, such as blasphemy. Naboth, who was unjustly accused of blasphemy (see 1 Kings 21), was carried out of the city and stoned to death. Stephen, in Acts 6, was also falsely accused of blasphemy and cast out of the city. And the Jewish Sanhedrin pronounced Jesus guilty of blasphemy because He called Himself the Son of God. So Jesus, the Son of God, became an outcast for calling Himself what He was.

Jesus willingly became an outcast so that we sinners, who have been justly cast out of Paradise by God, might be brought back into His presence. Jesus was thrown out of Jerusalem so that outcasts like us could be made citizens of the New Jerusalem, the eternal land of glory.

We read in Galatians that Jesus was made a curse to redeem sinners from the curse of the law. The living Word of God was made the curse of God. From a human perspective Jesus was unjustly condemned, but from God's perspective Christ was justly condemned, for He was paying for the sins of the guilty. That's why Hebrews 13:12 says, "Wherefore Jesus also, that he might sanctify the people with his own blood, suffered without the gate."

So Jesus, the cursed outcast, went to Calvary, carrying on His shoulders the cross, or at least the cross-beam, intended for Barabbas. The only-begotten Son of God the Father took the place of Barabbas (whose name means "son of the father") so that children of Adam might become the adopted sons and daughters of God. Picture Jesus, accompanied by His executioners, moving through Jerusalem with that heavy cross on His bloody back. Such an execution party usually would walk along the main streets of the city through its gates and squares and market places. The Romans wanted everyone to see this dark sight so they would refrain from law-breaking. So, the route to the place of execution was seldom the most direct way.

As a condemned man, Jesus was surrounded by four soldiers and preceded by another soldier who carried a placard stating the crime of which Jesus was found guilty. At a certain point, the execution squad realized that Jesus might collapse before He reached Calvary, so they looked for someone to assist with the load. They didn't want Jesus to die before they nailed Him to the cross.

The wonder of Jesus' love for His people is not only that for their sake He boldly faced death in His *strength,* but that He faced death for them in *utter exhaustion.* For an entire morning and afternoon, Jesus, while the anathema of His Father was descending upon Him, had to grapple with the forces of hell. He had to be crying out from His heart every minute, "Help me, Father. Give me strength to resist temptation. Help me to keep loving my persecutors."

The soldiers grabbed a man out of the crowd to help. It was Simon of Cyrene. Simon was an African from one of the most prominent port cities on the coast of North Africa. The Jewish faith had been established for centuries in Cyrene, and many of its Jewish converts visited Jerusalem, including Simon. Simon had come to Jerusalem to observe the Passover. He had probably saved his money to do so for years. Finally, he had enough to visit the temple where the Passover lamb would be slain.

God had other plans, however, for He would lead Simon to a different sanctuary than the temple. God would lead Simon to Golgotha, where the true Passover Lamb would be slain. God Himself would bring the Cyrenian Jew to encounter His only begotten Son, the Lord Jesus Christ—an encounter that would change this man's life. His identity would from this day forward be linked with Jesus Christ. He would be known as a coerced crossbearer who was conquered, by God's grace, to be made a willing crossbearer for Jesus.

A Coerced Crossbearer

Mark 15:21 tells us that the Roman soldiers compelled Simon to bear Jesus' cross. They "laid hold" upon him, that is, they pressed or drafted him for service (Luke 23:26). He was coerced into bearing Jesus' cross.

The word Mark uses here, translated as "compel," is found only twice in the New Testament, and in both cases it means coercion. The word actually derives from the Persian language, and suggested carrying out the orders of the Persian Emperor. Later, the word suggested being conscripted to fight for the state. Either way, the rulers of state, who are ordained by God, have the right to compel men to do things or to make sacrifices. Jesus Christ Himself, of course, was the true King. He has the right to exercise authority over all creation; He could command a fish to take a coin into its mouth and swim into a net. He could tell the wind to cease blowing. He could feed thousands of hungry people with a little boy's five loaves and two fishes. And He could ask for the foal of a donkey on which to ride into Jerusalem. People were constrained to obey Him.

But now, the very multitudes who had shouted "Hosanna" with such enthusiasm when Jesus rode into Jerusalem on the donkey's foal were accusing Him of being a criminal worthy of death on a cross. The soldiers of King Caesar, marching Jesus off to His death, were merely exercising their authority when they grabbed an African called Simon out of the crowd and yelled at him: "Carry this criminal's cross to Calvary! We are requisitioning you. We're going to make sure this deceiver gets every bit of the cross that He deserves."

Simon no doubt was ashamed, embarrassed, and angry. The edges of the heavy cross dug into his shoulders as he plodded after Jesus through the streets of Jerusalem. He was angry with the soldiers for seizing him, angry with this prisoner for not carrying His own burden, and angry because he knew that one who carried the cross of a condemned criminal would be considered unclean and therefore unfit for the Passover.

Being a Jew, Simon also knew that the cross was a shameful curse. Those who saw him would never forget that he had taken up the cross of the condemned Nazarene. To have come all the way from Cyrene to worship in the temple of his fathers and participate in the great Passover feast, to walk through the blessed streets Jerusalem, to meet believers he had not seen for years—then to have all these plans suddenly interrupted for such a bitter, degrading experience as crossbearing! How could he go home with nothing to tell except this story of how he had been insulted and shamefully treated?

Simon felt he was in the wrong place at the wrong time. If he had come an hour earlier, or an hour later, he could have missed this unholy procession. If he had walked a little faster, or a little slower, or taken another gate into the city, he would have missed it.

If only...if only...but no. In God's providence, Simon
was there at that place and at that time, and he carried Christ's cross.

What a contrast we have here! Simon was compelled to bear the cross of Jesus, who was willing to
bear the accursed cross for Simon of Cyrene. Jesus
willingly bore that wretched cross, even though
His body had nearly given way under it. Jesus had
endured the betrayal of Judas, the dark hours of
doubt at Gethsemane, the desertion of His disciples,
the mock trial before the Sanhedrin, abuse in the
palace of Caiaphas, Peter's denial, scourging, and
the sentence of death. He had lost a great amount
of blood. He'd had nothing to eat or drink since the
previous evening. And now this heavy cross was laid
on His shoulders. Physically speaking, it was a wonder that He could carry anything at all.

The soldiers recognized that the cross was too
heavy for Jesus. Yet who of all His friends stepped forward to share the burden? His disciples were nowhere
to be seen. Even the other Simon, Simon Peter—who
said he would go to prison and die before he'd forsake Jesus—was missing. All had forsaken Him. They
could not handle the cross. The cross was as much an
offense to them as it was to Simon of Cyrene.

What do you think was the heaviest weight on
Jesus as He bore that cross? It was not the weight of
the heavy wood on His shoulders, nor the absence of
His disciples; it was the wrath of God bearing down

upon Him. The heavy burden of the sins of all His people pressed Him to the ground.

The soldiers must have looked at Jesus and thought, "We cannot lose this one, for we have a sworn duty to perform." Little did they realize that, in their action, the heavenly Father was fulfilling His purpose, for if Jesus had succumbed before reaching the place of execution, the purpose of redemption would have failed. Just as God used angels to sustain Jesus in Gethsemane, so He used Simon to sustain Jesus along the *Via Dolorosa*, the way of sorrow, to His place of crucifixion. God used Simon to help His Son so that Jesus could achieve full satisfaction for the sins of His people by fully drinking the cup of the Father's wrath. So, though the soldiers meant this action for evil, God meant it for good.

Still, Simon had to be coerced to carry the cross; he did not willingly take it upon himself. By nature, we are all like Simon. We have no use for the cross of Jesus. We have no desire to bear that cross after Him. Why? Because the cross declares us guilty and condemned before God. And we do not want to hear that or believe it. We want to be smooth and sanitized Christians—not cross-carriers. The cross is an offense to us. The cross gets in our way. To take up Jesus' shame, Jesus' cross, and to follow Him is against our nature. It spoils our plans. It breaks our selfish utopias. It forces us to set priorities in our lives. It brings us face to face with ourselves and with God. The cross exposes us to who and what we are.

Have you ever followed Jesus with His cross on your shoulders, traveling, figuratively speaking, the way of sorrow to the place of crucifixion, all the while blind to what the cross does for you? You only wanted to escape the cross, not understanding that though men meant it for evil, God meant it for good.

What kind of a cross-carrier are you? Are you a coerced crossbearer or a conquered crossbearer?

A Conquered Crossbearer

Luke 23:26 adds one important detail to the account of Simon's crossbearing. It says, "On Simon they laid the cross, that he might bear it *after Jesus*." Thus, the heaviest end of the cross was either still on Christ's shoulders, and Simon took up the lower end of the cross, following after Jesus; or else, Simon took the entire cross-beam on his shoulders, providing Jesus some temporary relief. In either scenario, Simon followed behind Jesus every step of the way.

It appears that this encounter between a suffering Jesus and Simon of Cyrene was to Simon's eternal gain. We do not know how long it took before Simon became willing to bear Christ's cross, but many commentators believe it likely that somewhere along the way to Golgotha, Simon, like the centurion, was persuaded, "Truly this man was the Son of God" (Mark 15:39), and became one of the first Christian converts of Africa.

On what do commentators base this view? According to Mark 15:21, Simon was the father of Alexander and Rufus. We know from Scripture and historical records that Alexander and Rufus later became well-known leaders of the church at Rome. Mark wrote his gospel to the Gentiles, particularly for the Gentiles in Rome, who knew Alexander and Rufus. Tradition tells us that Rufus became a bishop in Spain and that Alexander died as a martyr. When the apostle Paul writes to the Romans he includes a greeting for Rufus. In Romans 16:13 he says, "Salute Rufus chosen in the Lord, and his mother and mine." Most likely, Alexander and Simon had died by that time. It appears that Simon spent the remainder of his life at Rome.

So why is this little note included in Mark's account of Jesus' crucifixion? Could it be, to let us know that, as a result of this encounter, Simon became a follower of the Lord Jesus, as did his sons? It seems that this encounter with Jesus Christ proved to be a blessing not only for Simon but also for his family.

Many of us are sitting here today because our predecessors crossed the path of a crucified Jesus. Time and again we see God's covenant faithfulness from generation to generation. From this simple statement, "Simon, the father of Alexander and Rufus," we learn that the crossbearing to which Simon was compelled most likely became a blessing to him and his family. How this should encourage us to take up crossbearing—not only for our own sake, but also for our children! If we love the Lord Jesus, then we must desire that all of our children's names be included with Rufus as "chosen in the Lord." And that is pos-

sible through the power of a sovereign God who is
delighted to work along covenantal lines as a faithful
God from generation to generation.

Dear parents, have you ever thought about how
your example in crossbearing might impact your
children for good and that they too might be like
Rufus—chosen in the Lord? I have been one of those
privileged children. I witnessed my parents carrying
their crosses after Jesus, and I've been the recipient
of untold prayers. I've heard my dad pray hundreds
of time, "Oh God, let us be an undivided family
reserved for the heavenly mansions above. For Lord,
we can't miss one of our children. They too must be
followers of Jesus. They too must bear the cross after
Jesus." Are you setting Christ-like examples for your
children and your grandchildren of what it means to
follow Jesus as a conquered crossbearer?

So what actually happened to Simon? Well, as
he was walking along behind Jesus, it seems to have
dawned on him that he might well be in the right
place at the right time. He probably entered into this
encounter with Jesus, thinking, "I've got to get out
of this somehow; I've got to save my life," but now,
as he follows Jesus at the expense of his own life, I
think the Holy Spirit began to show him who Christ
was and what He meant to poor sinners like him.
Simon probably began to understand Jesus' profound
answer to the question of how we can be saved: "If
anyone would come after me, he must deny himself
and take up his cross daily and follow me. For who-

ever wants to save his life will lose it, but whoever loses his life for me will save it" (Luke 9:23-24).

Moments ago, Simon may have thought he was the most unlucky man in the world, but now he may have begun to feel blessed. Isn't that what always happens when we begin to lose our life for Christ's sake? When I was fourteen, I remember complaining to my mom about being raised so strictly. How I resented that! Then the Lord converted me, and do you know what I thought? I thought that, of all the young people in the world, none was so blessed as I to have such caring, God-fearing, Word-centered parents. When I lost my life and was made willing to submit my life to Christ, I discovered that God graciously gave me godly parents whom He would use to train me to become more of a willing crossbearer who follows Christ.

Perhaps some of you are thinking even now that this is the wrong place and the wrong time, and that your time could be much better spent than listening to God's Word. But if your wrong-thinking, self-centered, self-preserving lifestyle is lost this moment for the sake of Christ, then your whole life will be saved for ever, and you will experience a joy and peace that the world cannot hold a candle to!

When we have an encounter with Jesus Christ, our lives are changed once and for all. Every time we hear the gospel, our path crosses the path of a crucified Jesus, who is now exalted and walks among us in the garments of the gospel. Each encounter will be either for our salvation or our damnation. It will soften or harden us—never leaving us exactly the same.

Your identity is linked with this crucified Jesus, for God has so ordered it that you would come under the ministry of the crucified and resurrected Lord Jesus this very hour and this very week. Oh, never forget that when you live under the gospel, Jesus Christ is passing by. Do you cry out for Him? Have you truly believed in Him alone for salvation? Are you bearing your cross after Him?

Even if those commentators are right who say that there is not enough proof in this history to indicate that Simon became a willing crossbearer, there is still a valid point in the method that has been described. There are still rich lessons in the beautiful picture of carrying Jesus' cross "after Jesus." There is no better way to bear a cross than to follow Christ's lead and example; in fact, there is no other way for a Christian to fruitfully bear his cross than to do so "after Jesus"—that is, to bear the cross as He bore His. God makes all His people willing to bear their crosses "after Jesus." That is God's purpose in bringing them into our lives; through crossbearing, we learn to look to the Lord Jesus Christ, to bear the shame of the cross, and to die to this world and all its expectations.

When the Lord converts us, He convicts us of sin. He makes us willing to flee to the crucified Jesus, who then becomes precious rather than offensive to us. Yet, in coming to the cross of Christ, which is our salvation, we soon learn that we must also bear the cross of Christ in sanctification. Simon did not initially understand the cross or its blessed purpose. But I think that God used his encounter with Jesus to teach him the necessity and purpose of the cross. We too must learn by the Spirit's teaching that we need to take up the cross and follow after Christ. We must bear God's sovereignly imposed crosses until God accomplishes His purpose with them.

How did Simon get to the place where God wanted him to be? Simon had to lose everything—his reputation, his Judaism, everything—to become a follower of Jesus Christ. But he gained more than he lost; he gained Christ and all His benefits. The Lord Jesus makes it plain that if we would follow Him we must be willing to die—to lose all our righteousness in order to follow Him alone.

This may raise several questions in your mind. First, is every believer destined to be a crossbearer? The Bible teaches us that since the Head of the church bore the cross, the body of the church has to bear the cross as well. Paul writes in 1 Thessalonians 3:3, "That no man should be moved by these afflictions: for yourselves know that we are *appointed thereunto*." Therefore, dear child of God, sooner or later, you will become a crossbearer. That is inevitable. The cross was inevitable for Jesus and is therefore inevitable for His children.

Dear believer, God compels you to become a bearer of the cross of Christ because He loves you.

He loves you with an everlasting love—and therefore, He makes you a bearer of the cross of Jesus Christ. Hebrews 12:6 says, "For whom the Lord loveth he chasteneth, and scourgeth every son whom he receiveth." Your crossbearing is evidence that you are a child of God. The apostle says that whoever is without chastening proves to be an illegitimate child, because God will never desert His own.

God gifts us with crosses so that we don't become spoiled children, but rather are trained and disciplined in the way of Jesus. And so, the fact that crossbearing is part and parcel of being a Christian should not be repulsive to us. We should welcome it, as hard as that is to do.

We are pilgrims here. God doesn't want us to put our tent stakes into this earth's soil too deeply. If we carry our crosses after Jesus, engage in Christian ministry, and testify openly against sin, you can be sure that we will face numerous crosses. You can't stand up for the name of Jesus and not bear the cross of Jesus. If our lives are spent for the cross of Christ, our lives will encounter that cross.

Be of good cheer: crosses are worth the price. A mother in our church recently had a baby after going through a very difficult time. She was in the hospital several times, but in the end received a beautiful baby. When I visited her, I said, "The Lord brought you through a deep way, didn't He?" "Oh," she said, "it's nothing. It's worth the price for this child in my arms." That's the way a Christian feels about Christ.

Whatever the crosses are, they are nothing with Christ in his arms. Christ is more than anything else and worth every price. He's worth living for. He's worth dying for. He's what life is. "For me to live is Christ, and to die is gain," Paul said.

So don't pity yourself as a Christian when you are called to bear crosses. Crossbearing is your road to crowning. Crossbearing is for your benefit; it is your Father's gift to you. Thank Him for maturing you in the faith through sovereignly designed, tailor-made crossbearing.

Secondly, when does God begin to put that cross on our shoulders? Usually, soon after He regenerates us. When He first draws us and when we are still weak in faith, He usually doesn't give heavy crosses. But as we grow in Christ, it usually doesn't take long before He weighs us down with heavier crosses. The cross can take many forms. It can be an outward, public burden; it can be some inward persecution, or some indwelling, persistent sin. It can be prodigal children, financial strain, disability, loss of work, strained relationships, battles with pride, or the loss of a loved one.

Dear child of God, how do you respond to the crosses in your life? When God brings affliction into your life, how to do you react? Hebrews 12:11 says, "No chastening for the present seemeth to be joyous, but grievous." Crossbearing is never pleasant. But the wonderful thing is that God leads His people in such a way that, step by step, slowly but surely, they become willing crossbearers. Eventually, they learn to confess like Job, "The LORD gave, and the LORD hath taken away; blessed be the name of the LORD" (1:21b).

If you're like me, such confessions seldom come as spontaneously as Job's did. They are often preceded by heavy bouts of murmuring, even rebellion. God sometimes has to bear down heavily on His people to make them willing to bear the cross of the Lord Jesus Christ. But one thing is sure: God's people will be willing in the day of His power.

Thirdly, what are some of the motives and purposes that God has for asking His people to bear the cross behind Jesus?

• *Conformity to Christ.* According to Romans 8:29, crossbearing is God's eternal means not merely to save you, but to conform you to His Son. The only way we begin to resemble the Lord Jesus Christ is when our flesh dies. In our lives, we show a mixture of godliness and fleshliness. In some ways, we resemble the Lord Jesus Christ; in other ways, we are so carnal! The Lord uses crosses to deliver us from our carnality and fleshly desires. His goal is not to make you comfortable in this world and to give you an easy journey to the heavenly Jerusalem, but to make you a holy man or woman, teenager, boy or girl. He wants to make you like His Son.

Hebrews 2:10 says: "For it became him (Jesus Christ), for whom are all things, and by whom are all things, in bringing many sons unto glory, to make the captain of their salvation perfect through sufferings." This is the way laid out for us as well. God wants to teach us to look to Jesus alone. That is why He takes away all the props in our life; only then will we learn to fetch all we need from Jesus Christ alone.

• *Obedience in Christ.* Crossbearing makes us willing to travel God's way. Simon was going his own way when he met Jesus, and likewise, we can feel rebellious when God's way conflicts with our plans. But if God lets us go our own way, we will miss the way of sanctifying obedience. We will not become partakers of Christ's holiness. So God says, "My child, you must go the way My Son's cross leads you; that's the only way you will become what I desire you to be. I want you to bear willingly My sovereignly imposed crosses until I accomplish My purpose with them. Only then will you be conformed to the image of My Son."

When we feel we lack the strength to pick up our cross, we must look to Jesus and obediently follow in His footsteps. Only then will we be able to endure the shame and rejection that comes with bearing it. Like Simon, we must follow Christ wherever He leads. That may be outside of the city to a place of shame and rejection, or it may be outside the camp, bearing the reproach of Christ. For as Jesus said, "If the world hate you, ye know that it hated me before it hated you. If ye were of the world, the world would love his own: but because ye are not of the world, but I have chosen you out of the world, therefore the world hateth you" (John 15:18-19).

• *Certification by Christ.* Be encouraged; your cross certifies your sonship and links you with Christ, who has a sanctifying purpose in mind for every cross you carry. He knows how difficult it is for your flesh; He knows how painful it is. But remember, He has measured out your every cross. He knows the way you take, but He also knows that it is the way that you must take. That is the way He has mapped out for you in your life so that you might draw close to Him, become like Him, abide in Him, and know that your sonship is sealed by Him.

• *Purgation through Christ.* Your cross proves that you are the gold of God's own choosing. The great Goldsmith is watching over you in your furnace of affliction until He sees His reflection in you. When Christ can be fully seen in you, the Lord will say, "It is finished. Now I will bring you to Myself; now you can be in My presence." Your future is not here; your life is not here; your joy is not in this world. You were redeemed for a better world, and this life is but the preparation by which God prepares you to be with Him.

Thus one reason we are still here in this world is because we are not yet fully purified for glory. There is a lot of carnality that has to be burned off in our lives. Remember, God will not leave His people here longer than necessary. When

His work is done and the work of the cross is done, then God will say, "Hitherto and no further; welcome home!"

• *Submission under Christ.* Dear child of God, as long as you are chafing under the cross and don't bear it joyfully, God will press down a little harder until you learn to acquiesce with your cross. You must embrace your cross. Pray to be like Samuel Rutherford; he learned so much in the school of Christ that when he saw another affliction coming, he'd say, "Here comes my Jesus!" And as Martin Luther used to say, "Letting God be God is half of all true religion."

The idea of crossbearing, of suffering shame for the name of Jesus Christ, is repulsive to many who assume that when they become followers of Christ, all will go well with them. They think they will no longer have pain, grief, or sorrow. But God never promises that to His people; He does not promise us heaven on earth. He tells us that our journey through life is a wilderness journey. Along the way we will have many tribulations, many sorrows, and much suffering—all to school us in the art of self-renunciation rather than self-pleasure.

• *The faithfulness of Christ.* Are you discouraged in your crossbearing? If so, remember that Jesus faithfully bore the heaviest part of your cross so you would not succumb under it. You may think at times that you cannot bear your burdens anymore or that they will crush you, but they never will. Look back in your life, dear believer. Has the Lord not always delivered you, lifted you up again, taken you out of the horrible pit and the miry clay, and established your goings (Ps. 40:2)? Jesus bore the heaviest part of the cross, the meritorious part—for He, not Simon, was nailed to the cross. That is why you will not collapse. He, the faithful High Priest, bore the cross for you. Will you not, out of gratitude, be willing to bear a lighter part of the cross for your dear Savior's sake?

• *The compassion of Christ.* Remember that when you bear your cross, Christ is moved with compassion towards your infirmity. The wonderful thing is that Jesus, who went to the cross for you, is now exalted at the right hand of the Father. One of the things He does as your compassionate High Priest is give you strength to follow in His footsteps. We need the powerful ministry of an exalted Jesus to follow in the footsteps of a crucified Jesus. He will teach you that without Him you cannot bear it, but with Him you can bear all things and, learning from Him, show compassion to those around you.

• *Growth in Christ.* Tell me, child of God, do you desire spiritual growth? God will answer that prayer by putting the cross on your shoulder. We learn most about ourselves, our sin, and our Savior in cross-bearing. God, His Word, and His promises become real through trials. That is why Paul says, "Now no chastening for the present seemeth to be joyous, but grievous: nevertheless afterward it yieldeth the peaceable fruit of righteousness unto them which are exercised thereby" (Heb. 12:11).

The Scriptures are plain: just as Christ would be ineffectual without the cross, so a Christian stagnates without a cross. When you murmur and chafe and rebel against your cross, you are not following your Master. You are denying your discipleship. You stunt your growth. You show your discipleship, your identity, and the genuineness of your faith only when you come after Him and bear His cross.

• *Joy in Christ.* Through crossbearing, we find joy in Christ alone. Crosses are imposed on all men— some bear them under protest, full of self-pity and resentment, complaining loudly along the way. True Christians are taught to embrace their crosses, call them blessings, and bear them without complaint, joyfully and even thankfully glorying in them as did Jesus Himself. Hebrews 12:1-2 says, "Let us run with patience the race that is set before us, looking unto Jesus the author and finisher of our faith; who for the joy that was set before him endured the cross, despising the shame, and is set down at the right hand of the throne of God."

God wants to lead you to the point where you begin to glory in the cross, counting it great joy when you may be a loyal servant of King Jesus under discouraging circumstances. He wants you to be like Ignatius, who counted his chains of suffering as pearls of joy because Christ counted him worthy to suffer for His sake. Ignatius could be so joyful because of "the joy that was set before him." And what joy is that? The joy of being with Christ, and of being delivered from this body of death!

Charles Simeon, preacher at Holy Trinity, Cambridge, for fifty-four years, was very discouraged for a time in 1796, feeling persecuted on all sides. "What's the use of going on?" he thought. He felt like resigning. But then he read Mark 15:21: "Simon bore his cross after Jesus." He was overwhelmed with joy, for he realized that God did not want him to resign, but to "re-sign"—to recommit, to bear his crosses with joy.

• *Preparedness for Christ in glory.* Through crossbearing, we are inclined to long more for the heavenly Jerusalem. We come to the point Paul reached when he said, "For to me to live is Christ, and to die is gain.... For I am in a strait betwixt two, having a desire to depart, and to be with Christ; which is far better" (Phil. 1:21, 23).

Oh, dear child of God, let these Christ-centered truths make you willing to bear your cross! Think of Christ and how He loved you. Think of how you should have been nailed on the cross and should have suffered God's undiluted wrath, but Jesus bore it in your place. Should that not motivate you then to bear the cross? Jesus wants to strengthen the bond of love for Him and glory in your soul. He wants His people to be bonded to Him and longing for their future home. Often He achieves that through crossbearing.

The apostle writes in Hebrews 13:13, "Let us go forth therefore unto him without the camp, bearing his reproach." And in 2 Corinthians 4:17 he reminds us, "For our light affliction, which is but for a moment, worketh for us a far more exceeding and eternal weight of glory."

So if you would be purified by taking up your cross and following after Christ, consider these final thoughts:

(1) Keep in mind that crossbearing is a blessed occupation. It brought Simon into Christ's company, it held him in Christ's footsteps, and it linked him with Christ's work. If your crossbearing brings you into Christ's company, Christ's steps, and Christ's work, you can be sure it is a great blessing for you. You can agree with the poet who wrote:

I think of the Cyrenian who crossed the city-gate
When forth the stream was pouring that bore
*   Thy cruel fate.*
I ponder what within him the thoughts that
*   woke that day,*
As his unchosen burden he bore that
*   unsought way.*
Yet, tempted be as we are; O Lord, was Thy
*   cross mine?*
Am I, like Simon, bearing a burden that is Thine?
Thou must have looked on Simon; turn, Lord,
*   and look on me,*
Till I shall see and follow and bear Thy cross
*   for Thee.*

(2) Let us be careful that our cross is not self-imposed. It must not be our cross, but Christ's cross. Too often, we make our own crosses rather than carrying Christ's cross. We can build a cross out of our legalism, our asceticism, our broken friendships, our sins—and then claim it is Christ's cross, when it is simply a cross of our own making. True soul-profiting crosses are ones Christ gives us. "Take *my* yoke upon you," He says.

Such crosses transform us and fit us for kingdom duty. The cross was placed on Saul of Damascus to bring the gospel to kings and Gentiles. It cost him all the energy of his life, but it turned a life of shame into a life of glory. Blessed are those of us who are transformed by the crossbearing of Christ to rejoice in persecutions for His name's sake.

(3) Dear unsaved friend, you too must become a crossbearer to prosper spiritually. You must bear the cross of Jesus after Him, because that is the path leading to the New Jerusalem. Don't say, "Well, I'm a nobody; why would God ever look on me?" Simon was a nobody, too. He was an unknown stranger in Jerusalem, a foreigner just passing by. But God gave him—not Peter, James, or John—the honor of carrying Jesus' cross. God can do great wonders for you, too. Today I invite you to take up your cross and follow Jesus Christ the Son of God. I invite you for your soul's sake to heed the voice of Jesus who said, "If

any man will come after me, let him deny himself, and take up his cross, and follow me" (Matt. 16:24).

The only cost of this amazing invitation is that you must die to your sinful self and to the ungodly pleasures of this world. Then, after you have followed Jesus like Simon of Cyrene did, you will one day hear Christ say on the Judgment Day, "Well done, good and faithful servant; enter into the joy of your Lord. You have cared for Me; you clothed and fed Me; you gave cups of cold water; you bore My cross."

Like the righteous, you may then ask in astonishment, "Lord, when saw we thee an hungered, and fed thee? Or thirsty, and gave thee drink?" (Matt. 25:37). And Christ will say, "Those who have done the will of the Father have borne My cross."

Walk as Christ walked. Bear the cross willingly, without complaint, and without shame. Keep your eyes on Christ, and on the joyful promise of His reward, the crown of life.

—2—

Jesus' Office-Bearing and Ours

A young wife once said to me in counseling, "My husband doesn't meet all my needs." When I explained that only Jesus Christ can meet all our needs, she was genuinely puzzled while her husband was genuinely relieved. Too often we Christians expect too little of Jesus and too much of each other.

The Lord Jesus is office-bearer *par excellence.* He alone can meet all our needs. Just as with cross-bearing, so with office-bearing: we can only be what Christ is calling us to be by partaking of Him and following His perfect example. Since we share in His anointing by faith, we also are called to reflect Him in His office-bearing. Thus, called to be office-bearers in His name, we must strive to meet each other's needs as much as possible in and through Christ as teaching prophets, interceding priests, and guiding kings. That's why the Heidelberg Catechism defines a Christian in terms of office-bearing that reflects the office bearing of Christ:

Question 32: But why art thou called a Christian?

Answer: Because I am a member of Christ by faith, and thus am partaker of His anointing; that so I may confess His name [that's our prophetical calling], and present myself a living sacrifice of thankfulness to Him [that's our priestly calling]; and also that with a free and good conscience I may fight against sin and Satan in this life, and afterwards reign with Him eternally, over all creatures [that's our kingly calling].

Let's consider Jesus' calling and ours in office-bearing through the lens of Luke 22:31-32: "And the Lord said, Simon, Simon, behold, Satan hath desired to have you, that he may sift you as wheat: but I have prayed for thee, that thy faith fail not: and when thou art converted, strengthen thy brethren."

We'll pursue our theme of "Jesus' Office-bearing and Ours" by examining three aspects of office-bearing embedded in our text: prophetic admonition, priestly intercession, and kingly commission. Sadly, all three of these subjects are often neglected today.

Prophetic Admonition

Jesus spoke the words of our text directly after He had instituted the Lord's Supper and eaten with His disciples. It's as if Jesus said, "I have seen that Satan is ready to attack you. Watch and pray that you don't enter into temptation, for Satan desires to have you." Jesus was confronting His disciples with the cruel temptations of the devil. He told all His disciples, but especially Peter, that Satan wanted to attack them and destroy them.

As the omniscient Prophet, Christ knew that Satan was trying to promote division among the disciples. Luke 22:24 says, "There was also a strife among them, which of them should be accounted the greatest." The frightening truth is that the disciples were not aware of Satan's presence; the comforting truth is that Jesus was. Jesus knew that when He, the Shepherd, would be smitten, the devil would redouble his energies and attack the disciples like a wolf attacks defenseless sheep to scatter them.

Jesus particularly warned Simon Peter that Satan had his sights set on him. J.C. Philpot wrote, "It's almost as if Satan says, I have gotten Judas; I will have Peter next. I have picked off one of the lieutenants; let me see if I cannot shoot down the colonel" (*Sermons,* vol. 1, p. 36). Satan always aims first of all for the most zealous followers of Christ, who testify like Peter, "Thou art the Christ, the Son of the living God" (Matt. 16:16). Peter was particularly vulnerable, not only because he was a leader among the apostles but because of his self-confidence. Peter had said, "Lord, even if I had to die with Thee, I would never be offended with Thee."

Peter was in serious danger because he saw no danger. He thought that he would carry on from strength to strength. He did not understand that

God's way is to make His strength perfect in our weakness (2 Cor. 12:9).

As the faithful, teaching Prophet, Jesus exhorts, "Simon, Simon," repeating His disciple's name with loving admonition, much like that of a parent. The repetition indicated special emphasis, grave concern, and tender affection. He addressed Peter twice, adding "behold," which is an additional warning to pay close attention. This emphatic warning was not only for Peter. The "you" in "Satan hath desired to have *you*" is second person plural, suggesting that Jesus was warning all the apostles as well as we who profess Him as Lord.

Those of us who are office-bearers in the church or at home are special objects of Satan's attention because of our past usefulness and our potential value for the cause of Christ. Ministers are among Satan's primary targets; Satan has declared *jihad* (a holy war) against us. He will use every weapon in his arsenal to destroy our ministries and to discredit the gospel of Jesus Christ. As Calvin says, the ministry "is not an easy and indulgent exercise, but a hard and severe warfare, where Satan is exerting all his power against us, and moving every stone for our disturbance" (*Commentary on John,* 2:288). Richard Baxter is even stronger: "Satan knows what a rout he can make of the troops if he can make the leader fall before their eyes. If Satan can ensnare your feet, your hands, your tongue, and make you

fall, your troops will scatter" *(The Reformed Pastor,*
BTT, 2001, pp. 74-75).

Satan attacks us at our weakest points. Like a good
fisherman, he baits his hook according to our appetites. I recently went on a fishing trip with my son,
and was pleasantly surprised to pull in a good-sized
walleye in the first five minutes. Later on, several
experienced fishermen told me that I shouldn't have
caught that fish with "only a worm." It wasn't the right
bait, but the fish was an easy catch. Far too often, we
are spiritually like my walleye—easy catches, even on
unsuitable bait.

We must be on our guard. We must expect sub-
tle temptations and violent assaults; we must set a
watch before every gate that leads into our heart.
What love Jesus showed to Peter, the apostles, and
to us in His warnings about such attacks! As Prov-
erbs 27:6 says, "Faithful are the wounds of a friend."
How we need to realize that "there is a spark of hell
in every temptation," as William Gurnall put it. J. I.
Packer said, "All Satan's temptations are so many
'welcome' billboards along the broad road that leads
to destruction."

Still, Peter brushed past the warning. He argued
in response, "Lord, I am ready to go with thee, both
into prison, and to death" (Luke 22:33). He was not
shaken by the seriousness of Christ's words and
apparently not even by the fall of Judas.

Simon, Simon, don't you see? Your intentions
are good, but do you not understand that Christ is

trying to warn you in love? Look inside, Simon. Cry out with the psalmist, "Search me, O God, and know my heart: try me, and know my thoughts: and see if there be any wicked way in me, and lead me in the way everlasting" (Ps. 139:23-24).

Today Jesus warns us also with prophetic admonition about Satan, the fallen angel who goes "to and fro in the earth" and is "a murderer and liar from the beginning." Satan is the Judas among the angels, the great apostate, the angel who rebelled against what God entrusted to him on the first day of creation. Satan has desired to have you, Jesus declares. "Desired" does not fully address the intensity of the Greek verb used here. *Exaiteo* is used here as an intensified form of the verb "to ask" or "to pray," which some have translated as "to ask excessively." Satan begged and pleaded for you; he put in his claims to have you and, as it were, sues God for you.

When Satan asked for Jesus' disciples, he was in effect saying, "Give me liberty to tempt Thy disciples, to try them by sifting, and I will prove my claim that they are nothing but hypocrites. I will prove they are no better than Judas, for they will all betray their Master. I request an opportunity to prove my claims against them. Only let me sift them and I shall prove that none of them—including their leader, Peter—are any different than Judas."

Satan wants to have you, too, dear young people. Satan is a real, living enemy, and he wants every one of us. Spurgeon said in his own day: "Certain theologians, nowadays, do not believe in the existence of Satan. It is remarkable when children do not believe in the existence of their own father." Knowing that he cannot defeat the Great Shepherd, Satan especially wants to have you, dear believer. He hopes to hurt Christ by damaging you as a member of Christ's flock.

The devil hates you because Christ is in you; you bear His image and love His appearance. You are the peculiar workmanship of God "created in Christ Jesus unto good works" (Eph. 2:10). By grace you have been snatched as brands from the burning fire and power of Satan. You have deserted Satan; you have fled his territory and deserted his army. By grace, you have acknowledged Christ as your Lord and Master, and confessed like Peter, "Thou art the Christ, the Son of the living God."

But Satan wants to sift you as wheat. He wants to do with you what a farmer does with his grain. In Bible times, a farmer's threshing floor contained both wheat and chaff; these had to be separated in order for the wheat to be useful in making bread. The broad instrument used to separate the wheat and chaff was called a sieve. The farmhand would take the sieve, fill it with a mixture from the floor, and shake it to the left and the right so that dust and dirt would fall through the sieve onto the ground. Then the worker would rock the sieve, raising one side and then the other. The wheat would settle in the sieve, while pieces of straw and chaff would come

to the surface. The worker would remove the pieces
of straw with his hand and blow off the chaff, leaving
nothing but pure wheat.

Now Christ says, "Satan desires to sift you as
wheat—to shake you violently back and forth, up
and down." You might say, "That doesn't seem too
bad; look at the pure wheat that results." But when
Satan sifts, his desire is not to purify you. Rather, he
wants to sift you so that you lose your faith, hope,
love, and strength. He wants to rock you so hard
that the graces God has worked in your heart will
be choked and strangled by the straw and chaff that
He brings to the surface. Satan wants to bring up the
evil remaining in your newborn soul to choke divine
graces, or better yet, prove that you possess little or
no wheat at all.

Not much good came to the surface when the
apostles were sifted in Satan's sieve. They all forsook
Jesus. Peter also denied his Lord, even with curses.
Other saints in the Bible did not do much better.
When Job, who was known for his piety and upright-
ness, was sifted by Satan, he cursed the day he was
born (Job 3:3). When Abraham, the father of the
faithful, was tempted, he lied about his wife, Sarah,
saying she was his sister. And Jacob said to God from
Satan's sieve, "All these things are against me" (Gen.
42:36). In such ways, even believers can show themselves to be more like chaff than wheat.

When we are in the sieve of Satan, we often do
no better. Old pieces of straw and chaff resurface in

us and threaten to choke out the wheat. The hour of temptation reveals how weak, proud, selfish, capricious, and unbelieving we still are and how easily we can backslide. Romans 7:18 becomes evident: in our flesh dwells no good thing.

How frightening Satan's sifting is when old sins that we thought were subdued and even destroyed are brought to the surface again! It seems as if everything the grace of God has worked in us disappears. We scan our hearts in vain for saving grace. Sometimes we can hardly claim a desire for God; at times, we can't even pray. In Satan's sieve, we can feel overpowered by sin. We fear that we will return to the world and our former life, and become, as Peter puts it, like a dog that returns to its vomit (2 Pet. 2:22). We ask apprehensively: Are we true believers or mere hypocrites?

Satan is no trivial enemy. John Blanchard says, "We are opposed by a cunning and resourceful enemy who can outlive us, outwork us, and outwit us." In his sieve, we learn more profoundly than ever that "the heart is deceitful above all things, and desperately wicked: who can know it?" (Jer. 17:9).

The Greek tense of our text implies that Satan wanted to do this sifting work now, just as the Shepherd was about to be removed from the disciples. How cunning Satan is in his timing; he does his best sifting when we miss the nearness and dearness of Christ. When sin dampens the exercises of faith or we feel spiritually depressed or forsaken, we find ourselves complaining like Job, "Behold, I go forward, but he is not there; and backward, but I cannot perceive him: on the left hand, where he doth work, but I cannot behold him: he hideth himself on the right hand, that I cannot see him" (23:8-9). In the midst of that uncertainty, Satan comes to do his sifting work.

In that sifting, what would remain of Jesus' flock? What would happen to Peter, to Thomas, to James? What will become of us? If our future depends upon our faith and our strength, we have little hope, for in our weakness we would remain unbelieving Thomases, return to our former life like Demas, or destroy ourselves like Judas. We would become Satan's prey, and he would devour us.

Priestly Intercession

Thank God our text doesn't end here. Jesus goes on to say to Peter and the rest of the disciples: "But I have prayed for thee, that thy faith fail not" (Luke 22:32a). Later Jesus spoke directly to Satan, saying, "This is your hour and the power of darkness" (v. 53). Jesus knew that he and Satan were in crisis. From the dawn of grace in Paradise, this crisis had been predicted. The battle of all battles between the seed of the serpent and the Seed of the woman was about to take place. And, as Genesis 3:15 predicted, Christ would bruise Satan's head, and Satan would bruise Jesus' heel.

The only way that Christ could bruise Satan's head and thereby defeat him was to leave His disciples behind and die on the cross for them. Only a God-man, sin-paying Surety could be the Savior and Advocate of His disciples. Jesus had to leave His disciples behind to be their atoning, interceding High Priest. The Shepherd had to be bruised to defeat the devil. To accomplish His great work of atonement, Christ had to tread the winepress alone (Isa. 63:3) and be smitten by the devil.

Christ anticipated His hours of sifting by the devil in three dreadful places: at Gethsemane, the place of Satan's hour; Gabbatha, the hour of Satan's evil coworkers; and finally, at Golgotha, where all the powers of hell would be unleashed. But before that happened, Jesus commended His disciples into the hands of His holy Father. Though no disciple was excluded, He told Peter specifically, now switching to the second person singular: "But I have prayed for *thee*, that *thy* faith fail not."

What a stark distinction there is between Satan and Jesus' requests. Satan pleaded for the disciples so he could tempt them and strangle grace in their life. This is the only prayer that Satan can pray: to tempt, to destroy, and to strangle. As accuser of the brethren, he could only pray for them to fall and then demand that they be cast into outer darkness.

Dear friends, as we listen to the claims of the devil, we must say with Luther, "We tremble, for so much of what the devil says is true. The devil has enough strength in his tail to knock my conversion out of me." Don't we all deserve outer darkness?

But the great High Priest also prayed, and His prayer was the opposite of Satan's in motive and content. The Greek verb in this verse allows the emphasis to fall on who is doing the praying. Jesus is saying: "I, yes, *I myself,* prayed." His prayer is a humble, personal plea, as a son asking something from a father. As the Son of the Father who loves His own, Christ out-desires, out-demands, and out-prays Satan in praying for the preservation of Peter and all His other disciples—then and now. "Father, keep them from the evil one" (John 17:15), He prays—what an eternal wonder of grace this is! Praise God that "we have an advocate with the Father, Jesus Christ the righteous: and he is the propitiation for our sins" (1 John 2:1-2). Dear believer, your divine Advocate, the Son of God, the ever-blessed Immanuel, pleads for you on stronger grounds and with stronger claims than the devil. He pleads on the grounds of His own sifting, His own bloody satisfaction, His own ransom price of sin. He not only asks, but demands, "Father, I will that they also, whom thou hast given me, be with me where I am; that they may behold my glory, which thou hast given me" (John 17:24).

When we hear Christ's pleadings on our behalf, we are filled with humble joy. With the apostle we cry out, "If God be for us, who can be against us? He that spared not his own Son, but delivered him up for us all, how shall he not with him also freely give us all things? Who shall lay any thing to the charge of God's elect? It is God that justifieth. Who is he that condemneth? It is Christ that died, yea rather, that is risen again, who is even at the right hand of God, who also maketh intercession for us" (Rom. 8:31-34).

This brings us to the heart of our text. To appreciate the necessity and beauty of Jesus as praying Advocate, we must experience some of the sifting of Satan. For it is especially in the sieve of Satan that we become personally acquainted with our precious Advocate who ever lives to make intercession for us (Heb. 7:25).

Notice carefully how Jesus prayed; He prayed that Simon's faith would not fail. The verb for "fail" is derived from *ekleipo,* which means "to come to an end," or "to give out." Our English word *eclipse* comes from this verb. Kenneth Wuest translates this verse, "That your faith should not be totally eclipsed." Jesus prayed that Peter's faith might not be eclipsed, be wiped out without a trace, or be overturned and die. He prayed that Simon's faith would make it through Satan's sifting and prevail *to the end.*

Christ did not ask the Father to prevent Satan's sifting. Jesus often allows the devil to sift us as wheat, under one condition: that our faith will not utterly fail. God had allowed Satan to sift Job, saying, "You may tempt and try him as you will, but touch not his life." Jesus is saying, "Satan, this is your hour to tempt and try My disciples as you will, but I will not give you power to remove the seed of faith, the essential wheat, from within them. I pray to My Father, who is mightier than you, that their faith fails not."

Satan's desire is to overturn and destroy our faith by choking it with impurities, but Christ's desire is to strengthen our faith by purging the wheat. He desires to purify the grains of divine grace so that the chaff may be destroyed and our faith prevails.

What's more, Satan had to ask God's permission to sift the disciples as wheat. Christ overrules Satan. He sets limits beyond which Satan is not allowed to go. Satan may take away much through sifting. He can destroy much through his sieves of prosperity and adversity, and he can wreak havoc through his sieves of spiritual temptation and difficulty and fear. As William Gurnall says, "No actress hath so many dresses to come in upon the stage with as the devil hath forms of temptation."

Satan can destroy much in sifting us. He can destroy our fleshly self-confidence, fleshly expectation of an earthly kingdom, fleshly holiness, fleshly pride, fleshly strength, fleshly wisdom, fleshly prayer, and fleshly self-righteousness. All that is self must fall as dust or dirt through the sieve. But the one thing that Satan cannot destroy is our non-fleshly, divine, saving faith. He cannot touch that noble grace by which we are united to Christ. He cannot touch faith, which is that bond of union by which Christ dwells in our hearts. He cannot destroy the faith that works by love, produces hope, and is the heart of true godliness. The faith that cleaves and clings to the Lord, that cannot but love God, that hangs upon Christ and God's promises in Him, cannot be destroyed by

Satan. Satan cannot destroy that faith which clings to God's Word and which seems the humblest of all graces though it is the most important grace of all, for it is the foundation and support of every grace.

As the winds blew and the waves roared around Noah's ark, so the storms of temptation will rise against the church. But she is a militant church. God brings His work into the sea. He uses the devil to destroy what must be destroyed in the church. Through satanic sifting under the permissive and governing guidance of God, we learn how weak and frail we are. As the Heidelberg Catechism says, "We are so weak in ourselves, that we cannot stand a moment." But that weakness forces us to cast ourselves upon our intercessory High Priest to preserve us in the midst of the sea.

This High Priest never fails. Satan sifts to destroy the wheat and save the chaff in us, but Christ overrules so that the wheat is saved and the chaff destroyed. He reaches into the sifting process, removing the straw with His hand and blowing off the chaff with His mouth. Satan would sift true life out of us, but Christ sifts out only what needs to die so that we learn to say with Job: "The LORD gave, and the LORD hath taken away; blessed be the name of the LORD" (Job 1:21).

Christ turns all of Satan's sifting on its head, so that it works together for our good and growth. Because of Christ's intercession, Peter would not be like Judas and hang himself; he would repent.

Thomas would not sink away in unbelief but be delivered. The gates of hell will not prevail against a single believer, for no one can pluck them out of Christ's hands nor out of the hands of His Father. As priestly Advocate *(parakletos),* Christ has carved the names of believers upon the palms of His hands. Satan asks for permission to sift us, but Christ has earned the right to use Satan's sifting for the healing and eternal salvation of His own. As Calvin put it, "Even the devil can sometimes act as a doctor for us."

Dear child of God, you will not perish at the hand of Satan because of your own evil heart. Perhaps right now you are in Satan's sieve, and you came here this morning with Esther's confession on your lips: "If I perish, I perish, but I will go in to the King of kings." The waters of afflictions may threaten to drown you, but remember, your faith has not been fully eclipsed. Your interceding Advocate is still upholding your faith, even in the midst of strife. Oh, be comforted by knowing that the Savior who prays that your faith will not fail assures you that the Father *always* hears those prayers (John 11:42).

Be of good courage. The Lord is faithful. He will honor His own work as priest. As 1 Corinthians 10:13 says, "There hath no temptation taken you but such as is common to man: but God is faithful, who will not suffer you to be tempted above that ye are able; but will with the temptation also make a way to escape, that ye may be able to bear it."

The Lord will not lose a single one of His own, no

matter how hard Satan sifts. For Job 23:10 assures us that even the least shall come forth purified, as gold. And God promises in Amos 9:9 that despite our being sifted, "yet shall not the least grain fall upon the earth."

Kingly Commission

We have seen Christ's prophetic admonition to the apostles and His priestly intercession on behalf of Peter. Now, let us consider His kingly commission to Simon Peter when He said, "And when thou art converted, strengthen thy brethren" (Luke 22:32b).

Peter was sifted and he fell. Though the Lord allowed it, Peter's fall was entirely his own fault. But Peter also repented, returned to Christ, and believed in Him as the only One who could preserve him. In the sieve of Satan, our work is destroyed but God's work is purified. Nothing is left but a poor, wretched sinner who casts himself upon the righteousness of Christ. That is always the purpose of God.

How rich believers are, for they have a work within them that will never perish, thanks to the work of Christ. Satan put in a claim for Christ's disciples, but Christ put in a counterclaim. With His calm, majestic, kingly commission, Christ retained His supremacy over Satan. For Christ's sake, mercy triumphs in the face of justice. As the commentator J.P. Lange says: "The holy supplication of mercy countervails before God the daring appeal of the accuser." Peter never would have repented if left to himself. But one look from Christ was sufficient; the disciple who had denied his Lord went out and wept bitterly (Matt. 26:75). What clearer proof could there be but repentance to show that the seed of faith implanted in Peter was not dead? Repentance and faith are inseparable (Acts 20:21); repentance is an act and profound expression of faith.

Genuine repentance involves four things: (1) spiritual enlightenment and remembering whence you have fallen; (2) confessing, grieving over, and forsaking sin; (3) bowing under sin's just judgment, which is death, and (4) falling upon Christ for mercy. Peter still would have confessed Christ as righteous even if Christ had not restored him. But Christ wondrously chose to restore Peter. Soon after Christ rose from the dead, the angels told the Jesus-seeking women: "Go tell his disciples *and Peter* that he goeth before you into Galilee: there shall ye see him" (Mark 16:7).

So certain was Peter's repentance that Christ gave Peter a royal commission: "*When* (not *if*) thou art converted (that is, 'turned again' or 'repentant'), strengthen thy brethren." This declarative *when* is the word of a King who knows He has power over Satan. "Where the word of a king is, there is power" (Eccl. 8:4). Christ sees that Satan is mighty and that Peter will fall, but He knows that His own royal power is almighty. He is the loving, almighty King of kings! As His Father's King to whom all power is soon to be given, He commissions Simon Peter even as He

Himself is about to plunge into the depth of suffering and Peter into the depth of his sin.

But hadn't Peter already been converted and been brought to repentance? Yes, but now he would learn repentance at a deeper level. He would be more profoundly broken this time. He would lose all self-reliance and become nothing but a sinner before God.

But the wonder of grace is that when Peter repented and thought he was good for nothing, he actually became more fruitful and serviceable than before, for the Lord delights to use broken vessels. A.W. Tozer says: "God will not use a man greatly until He has broken him deeply."

Oh, what grace Peter would experience when Christ presented this royal commission to him privately (Luke 24:34), then later in the presence of some of the apostles (John 21). Then Peter would receive strength as a teaching prophet to admonish others in love, as an intercessory priest to pray for others in love, and as a guiding king to strengthen others in love in the ways of Christ.

But precisely how would he strengthen the brethren? In many ways:

(1) By declaring the bitterness of sin in denying his Master.

(2) By emphasizing the weakness of the flesh, our need for continual dependence on God and for lifelong repentance and humility of heart.

(3) By admonishing others about Satan's wiles and the need to watch and pray against them.

(4) By declaring Christ's willingness to meet all our needs through His prophetical admonitions, His prayers, and His love to backsliders.

(5) By unveiling the love of Christ in declaring His kingship *before* the prophesied offense was committed.

(6) By teaching the joy of restoration.

When a bone is broken and reset, it can become stronger than before. The strength of healing would be evident in Peter's preaching on Pentecost and later in his exercise of church leadership. Perhaps that strength is evident most of all in Peter's epistles, which are filled with love, tenderness, admonition, guidance, and encouragement. Having experienced the cunning of Satan and the indestructible fidelity of Christ, Peter could become a testimony to others through his unmatched First Epistle, by means of such texts as 1 Peter 5:8, "Be sober, be vigilant; because your adversary the devil, as a roaring lion, walketh about, seeking whom he may devour." He could offer assurance to those "who are kept by the power of God through faith unto salvation ready to be revealed in the last time" (1 Pet. 1:5).

With the possible exceptions of Paul and John, no one was used in the New Testament church like Peter to comfort and strengthen the brethren. Like Paul, Peter could say after his repentance and restoration, "To the weak I become as weak, that I might gain the weak" (1 Cor. 9:22). He could now feed both little lambs and mature sheep (John 21:15-17). Before, he would have beaten the little lambs.

So, the Lord used Simon Peter's denial for his own good (Rom 8:28), to humble him and to strengthen his Christian brothers. Because of that sifting, Peter would better serve the New Testament church as a teaching prophet, interceding priest, and guiding king, gaining his strength from the supreme Office-bearer who would meet all his needs.

Our Office-bearing

Office-bearing is our calling still today. If we are true Christians, we are to be office-bearers in this world to our spiritual brothers and sisters in faith through the power of Christ. Of course, our office-bearing is not on a par with that of Christ. We are not omniscient prophets who foretell future events, but we are called to teach the gospel to others and to confess the name of Christ. We are not called to be priests who sacrifice ourselves to merit forgiveness of sin from God, but we are called to live sacrificial lives of thankfulness to God and to intercede for others. We are not called to be kings like Jesus to whom all power in heaven and earth was given, but we are called to fight against sin and Satan and to strengthen fellow believers.

Let's return to the Heidelberg Catechism's definition of a Christian: "I am a member of Christ by faith, and thus am partaker of His anointing; that so I may confess His name, and present myself a living sacrifice of thankfulness to Him; and also that with a free and good conscience I may fight against sin and Satan in this life, and afterwards reign with Him eternally, over all creatures."

Do you possess the marks of a true Christian, according to the Catechism? Are you, first, "a member of Christ by faith"? A true Christian is a member of the body of which Christ is the Head. A true Christian belongs to Christ by faith. The very word *Christian* means *belonging to Christ*. You cannot be a Christian without belonging to Christ.

Second, are you a "partaker of Christ's anointing"? Union with Christ is possible only through the Holy Spirit. The same Spirit that anoints Jesus anoints the believer. That is why the office-bearing Christian can say, "I am a partaker of His anointing." Christ gives His Spirit to each of His children so they may be anointed, guided, instructed, and led by the same Spirit that anointed the Lord Jesus Christ.

Third, are you striving to fulfill your calling as God's prophet, priest, and king? These offices, which were lost in Paradise, are restored to us through the Spirit's anointing and uniting us with the Lord Jesus Christ. A true Christian confesses Christ's name as prophet, offers himself as a living sacrifice to Christ and intercedes on behalf of others as priest, and strengthens others and reigns forever with Christ as king.

Do you confess Christ's name to others as prophet? Do you, like Christ, speak a word of prophetical admonition, based on Scripture, to family members, friends, neighbors, and strangers? Do you speak to those sitting next to you on an airplane? So many people really do want to unveil their hearts, but we, sadly, are often too preoccupied to notice or too timid to draw them out. Do you strive to confess Jesus' name with your whole life, in your conversation, your walk of life, and the way that you handle yourself?

Do you present yourself as a living sacrifice of thankfulness to Christ with a priestly heart? Does your life reflect the opening verses of Romans 12: "I beseech you therefore, brethren, by the mercies of God, that ye present your bodies a living sacrifice, holy, acceptable unto God, which is your reasonable service" (vv. 1-2)? Do you consecrate to Jesus all of your energy, time, and talents in the home, school, and business? Do you pledge allegiance to Christ in everything you have—your money, your possessions, your very thoughts? Are you a priestly intercessor for other believers? Do you pray that their faith will not fail? Are you praying for revival and the worldwide coming of Christ's kingdom?

Our best friends are those who pray for us. John Newton said that when he became discouraged, one of his greatest comforts was knowing that someone somewhere in the world was lifting up his worthless name and lisping it in the ears of the Lord of Sabaoth, who in turn would intercede with the Father on Newton's behalf. What prayer-warriors we ought to be!

Do you reach out to the underprivileged in your community? I have a friend who hands out John Blanchard's *Ultimate Questions* on the streets of Capetown, South Africa, six days a week, all day long. He lives in a little two-room apartment. His major expense is buying tennis shoes. Last year, he wore out more than a dozen pair of them. Sometimes people respond with abuse—verbal abuse or eggs thrown in his face. His life is a priestly sacrifice. Obviously, we can't all do this on a full-time basis, but we can ask ourselves: What am I sacrificing for Christ, out of gratitude for His salvation? Are you denying yourself in any way for Him?

Finally, do you serve Christ as king by strengthening your fellow believers, by fighting against sin and Satan, and by anticipating reigning with Him eternally? The true Christian by grace will overcome the world, the devil, and sin, because Jesus has overcome them all. And one day all Christians will be gathered to the true Christ forever to be with their King of kings in glory.

Charles Spurgeon tells the story of a king's young son who was caught by a courtier in the king's throne-room trying on the king's crown. The courtier feared that the boy would soon try to overthrow the king, but the king was not worried: "I rejoice that my son is putting on his future crown already, for he is heir to the throne." Spurgeon then went on to say that believers should try on their future crowns now, recognizing that they are adopted sons of the King of kings and will one day reign with Him.

Whom are you serving? When I was sixteen, my nineteen-year-old brother announced to me that he had discovered what life was all about and could summarize it in one word: *service.* He went on to say, "God created us in Paradise to serve Himself and our neighbor. We destroyed that. Through regeneration, repentance, and faith in Christ, He restores us as prophets, priests, and kings to serve Him. So our goal in life ought to be to serve God and to serve man, and therefore, the only way we can be truly happy is when we fulfill the purpose for which God made us. Service will reap genuine joy."

My father, who was a carpenter, put it this way. "Son, you wouldn't use a saw to nail home a nail or a hammer to saw a board, but you would use the tools for the purpose they are designed to fulfill; so God would not have us live to ourselves, but unto Him and to our neighbor." When we live for ourselves, we are trying to nail home a nail with a saw; it doesn't work. That's why the more affluent and self-centered societies in the world become, generally speaking, the more unhappy they become. We need to live office-bearing lives of service. We are called to be prophets, priests, and kings to God.

Let us return from every backsliding way, and turn to the living God. Dear believer, when you are brought back from backsliding, do you speak of that to others? Do you share your experiences in humility and gratitude to Christ for restoring you? Let us not forget what great battles go on in the invisible world over our poor souls. Let us tell others how Christ's constant intercession keeps our faith from being eclipsed and our souls from falling into hell.

Strengthen your brethren. Be a counselor to wanderers. Tell them what a bitter thing it is to depart from the living God. Warn them of the devices of Satan. Admonish them about the seriousness of life and the certainty of judgment. Tell others how worthy our King is to be served, feared, loved, and worshiped. If you are a preacher of the gospel, you can tell the worst criminal that he matters to God. And when the criminal responds, "Why do you bother with me?" you have every right to say: "Because you are of great value, for you have a never-dying soul, and a great Savior is willing to save it." A true preacher knows that every soul is more valuable than all the riches of this world. Proclaim the good news that Christ has no pleasure in the death of sinners but wills that they should turn unto Him and live.

Warn the unconverted that if they are not purified by Christ, they will be sifted to damnation by Satan. Warn them in love that if they have never experienced the sifting of Satan and been brought to Christ through it, they will be placed in Satan's sieve forever on account of unforgiven sins and an unbelieving heart.

Dear young people, Satan especially desires you, for you are the future of the church and of society.

Oh, do not be enticed by him who wants to destroy you; rather, respond to Christ who desires your salvation and invites you, "Incline thine ear and come unto me; hear and thy soul shall live, and I shall make an eternal covenant with you, even the sure mercies of David" (Isa. 55:3).

When you enter Satan's sieve, pledge your allegiance to Christ rather than to Satan. Only then will your faith prevail. Pray that you may remain one of those who can respond to Christ's question, "Will ye also go away," by saying, "Lord, to whom shall we go? Thou hast the words of eternal life" (John 6:67-68).

I close by leaving you with two pieces of advice:

First, flee every day to Christ as your teaching Prophet, interceding Priest, and guiding King. He is your only hope and stronghold. Only in Christ and through His Word can you overcome Satan. Go ahead and condemn yourself as severely as Satan condemns you, but then bring your failures to our precious Advocate, and He will restore you in forgiveness and love.

Second, defy Satan with the Word of God. Stand fast; do not compromise with him, but gird yourself with all the armor of God (Eph. 6:10-20). Do not give way to despair in his sifting; remember, Satan is chained. He wants to claim you; but Christ's claim upon you is stronger. So be hopeful, sober, and vigilant. Be neither self-confident nor overly fearful, but stand guard against the wiles of the serpent. Remember that your Savior prays for you that your faith won't fail. And remember the promise of Romans 16:10, that "the God of peace shall bruise Satan under your feet shortly. The grace of our Lord Jesus Christ be with you. Amen."

3

Jesus' Tears and Ours

We are all touched by tears. They can touch us with great power, whether or not we know the story behind them. Some tears are selfish and terribly sinful; some are selfless and wonderfully righteous. What makes you cry?

We read of Jesus' tears three times in the Bible. Let us study Jesus' tears, then examine our own tears and ask: Am I moved to tears by the same things that moved Jesus? Am I walking as He walked?

The three texts that we will look at are John 11:35, which says, "Jesus wept"; then Luke 19:41, which says, "And when he was come near, he beheld the city [i.e., Jerusalem], and wept over it"; and Hebrews 5:7, which says, "Who in the days of his flesh, when he had offered up prayers and supplications with strong crying and tears unto him that was able to save him from death, and was heard in that he feared."

We will consider Jesus' Tears and Ours in three ways: Jesus' tears at Bethany, Jesus' tears over Jerusalem, and Jesus' tears in Gethsemane.

Jesus' Tears at Bethany

The fact that Jesus wept teaches us three things about our Savior. First, Jesus' tears prove His *complete humanity*. Physically and psychologically, Jesus was as human as you and I. His sinlessness did not diminish His humanity. His tears showed how human He really was: He had eyes, tear ducts, and cheeks down which tears could run.

Second, Jesus' tears show us that He had, as the Westminster Confession of Faith tells us, a *"reasonable soul."* He had a human mind and human thoughts. Behind His tears were thoughts and emotions. He had reason to weep as well as the capacity to weep.

Third, in addition to His humanity and reasonable soul, Jesus' tears tell us that He was the *Son of God* in human flesh. In Him we see the God who was, and is, and is to come. "He that hath seen me hath seen the Father," Jesus said in John 14:9. Just as the Father is revealed by the works Jesus accomplished with His hands, so the Father is revealed in the tears that Jesus shed. Jesus' tears show us what kind of divine being God is.

But why did Jesus weep? What does His weeping mean for us? What do His tears say about Him? In John 11:35 we read of Jesus' tears at Bethany. What were those tears all about?

First, they were tears of *sympathy*. Lazarus had died, and his sisters, Mary and Martha, were grieving. So were their friends who came to sympathize with the women in their loss. Verse 33 says, "When Jesus therefore saw her [Mary] weeping, and the Jews also weeping which came with her, he groaned in the spirit, and was troubled." In the midst of people who were weeping, Jesus also wept.

It is surely part of human nature to be affected by what happens to other people. The closer our relationship with them and the deeper our love for them, the greater the grief that we share with them when they suffer loss. We are told in verse 5 of this chapter that "Jesus loved Martha, and her sister [Mary], and Lazarus." His tears show that He had compassion on these sorrowing sisters.

On another occasion, recorded in Luke 7, Jesus and His disciples were approaching the city of Nain when they saw a funeral procession coming toward them. A widow whose only son had died was following the corpse. Luke 7 tells us, "When the Lord [Jesus] saw her, he had compassion on her, and said unto her, Weep not" (v. 13). Jesus then reached out to touch the coffin and commanded the young man to rise. The dead boy came back to life and sat up.

Jesus had *compassion* on the grieving widow. He did not merely act on her behalf; He also responded emotionally to her need. He did not simply analyze the situation, conclude that, as the incarnate Son of God, He had the power to raise the boy, and therefore did it to show that He was the Son of God. No, He acted because He had compassion on the sorrowing widow. He was deeply moved by the plight of the

woman who had lost her only son and now was left
without any means of support. Jesus stepped into
the widow's situation, put Himself under her burden,
and reached out to help her.

Likewise, Jesus' tears at Lazarus's graveside were
signs of genuine sympathy. They reveal the nature
of Jehovah, the true God, of whom Psalm 103:14
says, "He knoweth our frame; he remembereth that
we are dust." God the Father is not aloof and distant
and unconcerned. He is the One who stoops to save;
that is why He sent His Son to earth. Jesus' compassion is a sign of the tender mercies of Jehovah. Even
now, though Jesus no longer walks the earth in His
human nature, He is still touched by our infirmities,
as Hebrews 4:15 says. He is compassionate and kind,
amazingly, tenderly, and repeatedly.

If you think that God does not care about your
sorrows and that Jesus is insensitive to your suffering,
your concept of God needs correction. Perhaps dull-
ness, blindness, or unbelief makes you feel this way.

We are told that "Jesus wept." The message of
those two words is that God cares for us. As Hebrews
4:15 says, "He is touched with the feelings of our
infirmities." He is a High Priest who senses our need
and responds to it. He felt our every sin on Golgotha's hill, and now He feels our every affliction at
the Father's right hand. Oh, what a wonder it is to
say, "He is my brother in adversity, my companion
in sorrow, my friend in affliction, and my strength in
weakness. Jesus carries my name and my cause on

His high-priestly heart and high-priestly shoulders. My name is engraved on His high-priestly hands. He will never forsake the work of His own hands." Jesus is exactly the Savior we need. He is not only the transcendent Son of God (Heb. 4:14) but also the immanent Son of man (Heb. 4:15).

And so you are urged to go to your Savior just as He is and just as you are, with all your sins. Ask Him to show His care, concern, and kindness to you in all your difficulties, and you will find that He will exceed all your expectations. His sympathy is immeasurable.

What about your tears; are they motivated by sympathy for those in need? Are you truly touched by their circumstances? Does your heart go out to the mourning, the needy, the handicapped, the lost? Do you have a big evangelistic heart? Are you walking as Jesus walked?

The tears that Jesus shed at Bethany were not primarily tears of sympathy, however. There is another emotion referred to in these verses, and it is summed up in the word *groaning*. Verse 33 tells us that Jesus "groaned in the spirit." He shed tears of groaning. What does that mean? Let us look closer at the situation that prompted the groaning. Mary and the Jews were weeping, but we are told that Jesus first "groaned in the spirit and was troubled" (v. 33). After that, He wept.

The friends of Mary and Martha responded to Jesus' tears by saying, "See how He loved him!" They understood those tears as tears of sympathy. Yet some questioned the depth of that sympathy, saying, "Couldn't He have prevented this man from dying, since He could open the eyes of the blind?" Jesus' reaction to that question was more groaning. Verse 38 says, "Jesus therefore again groaning in himself cometh to the grave."

The Greek word used here for *groaning* is only used a few times in the New Testament. Each time it is used, it implies disapproval. So it is used here. Jesus wept in sympathy but also in antipathy to the attitude of the mourners. When Jesus groaned in His spirit, He was manifesting a different attitude from those who were weeping. It was an attitude of opposition.

The word for groaning was also used in reference to the snorting of horses. When soldiers rode into battle on the backs of horses, the horses sniffed the fight and stormed into the midst of the fray. Likewise, when the Lord Jesus Christ groaned, it was not the type of wailing exhibited by Mary and Martha and their friends. Jesus did not wail. He groaned, but not in a show of grief that others saw. Rather, He groaned in His spirit because of the turbulence and unrest within Him. His groaning was that of anger; His tears were those of indignation.

Jesus groaned because He saw the tears and sorrow of His friends and realized how limited their faith was. Martha and Mary each had told Jesus, "If Thou hadst been here, our brother would not have died." The implication was that, because Lazarus had died, everything was over. There was nothing more to do but dismiss the mourners, who may have been professional mourners with no faith at all in Jesus.

So Jesus wept, but with tears of anger—first at the limited faith of Mary and Martha. Then, when He came to the tomb where Lazarus was buried, Jesus groaned again. Perhaps He groaned because of divine anger at the limited understanding of those who believed in Him and should have trusted Him more, even in death. Perhaps He groaned because of divine hostility to sin and death and Satan.

But His tears also indicated anger against the enemy who had caused death. Into the world that God had made "very good," and into those human beings made in God's image and likeness and for His fellowship, Satan had sown sin and death. Satan ruins life, and he does it by tempting us to sin. Yet here stands the Christ, who came to this world to oppose sin and death. Here is the seed of the woman who is going to bruise the serpent's head.

> *When all was sin and shame,*
> *The second Adam to the fight*
> *And to the rescue came.*

The Son of God came to this earth that He might destroy the works of the devil. As Jesus stood at the grave of Lazarus, surrounded by people who wept and wailed, He fortified Himself, then rushed like a horse into the battle against death.

Death still causes weeping and wailing. The

prophet Isaiah spoke of a veil of mourning over the face of the nations. However much you and I may try to make the most of our time here on earth, we know that one day we will die. Death reminds us that we are frail and fallible. It stalks us. It makes us afraid because we are sinners and have fallen from grace. We may go through this life looking for fun, pretending that we have nothing to fear, but whenever we hear about someone dying, we are reminded that we will also die. We try to stifle our fears and silence our guilt, but we are already defeated. All of us will die.

What will you do about death? There is nothing you can do to avoid it. It does not matter who we are or how high up the ladder we have climbed. Death brings us down. We had nothing to say about the day of our birth, and we have nothing to say about the day we die. Death is the enemy that has already won. The sin within us makes us fear death because dying will bring us into the very presence of God. And how can we deal with that?

We cannot face death alone. We need a mighty Savior. We need someone who will act for us, not merely feel for us. Jesus does feel for us as no one else can, but that is not enough. We also need someone to take on the enemy of death and fight for us. When Jesus stood before the tomb of Lazarus, weeping tears of anger, He was showing us how He had come to earth to fight death for us. He came to take on the enemy. He came to deal the deathblow to death and to bring everlasting life to repentant sinners.

So Jesus, groaning in spirit, came to the tomb, which was a cave sealed off by a large stone. And He prayed, "Father, I thank thee that thou hast heard me. And I knew that thou hearest me always: but because of the people which stand by I said it, that they may believe" (vv. 41-42). Then, to make it clear that God would respond to His anger against unbelief and sin and death, Jesus cried out, "Lazarus, come forth!"

And Lazarus walked out of the grave. He that was dead "came forth bound hand and foot with grave-clothes" (v. 44), thereby proving that Jesus is the Conqueror of sin and death and the grave. Eternal life is in His hands.

Oh, what a Savior! He not only weeps tears of tender sympathy and of groaning anger, but is also victor over sin and death and hell. If you do not believe in this Savior, I urge you to repent of your sin and trust in Him before it is too late. If you continue to reject and grieve the Son of God, you may be sure that the triune God will groan against you on the Day of Judgment. I warn you in love: Do not grieve the Son, do not step upon the heart of the Father, do not vex the Holy Spirit. Do not rest short of a saving relationship with the Triune God. "Kiss the Son, lest he be angry and ye perish from the way, when his wrath is kindled but a little. Blessed are all they that put their trust in him" (Ps. 2:12).

For you who believe in the Son, do you ever shed tears of anger over sin and its consequences? Do you shed tears of anger over seeing thousands persist in rejecting Jesus to their own damnation?

Jesus' Tears over Jerusalem

But Jesus shed other tears. We see in Luke 19:41 that He also wept over Jerusalem. What kind of tears were these? The word that Luke uses is the same word that John used for the weeping of Mary and the Jews. When He drew near to the city, He *wailed* over it. These were tears of *anguish* and *lamentation*.

Jesus wept over Jerusalem because of what He saw hovering over her. He cried out, "If thou hadst known, even thou, at least in this thy day, the things which belong unto thy peace! but now they are hid from thine eyes" (v. 42). Matthew 23:37-38 quotes Jesus saying, "O Jerusalem, Jerusalem, thou that killest the prophets, and stonest them which are sent unto thee, how often would I have gathered thy children together, even as a hen gathereth her chickens under her wings, and ye would not! Behold, your house [your temple] is left unto you desolate."

Jesus wept tears of anguish for Jerusalem's sinners, who were making three fatal mistakes:

First, *they had not realized their day.* "Thou knewest not the time of thy visitation," says verse 44, meaning that the inhabitants of Jerusalem were ignorant of their incredible opportunity to marvel at the very Son of God come to earth. The wonder of God's love, mercy, and power were being displayed as never before, and all for their good—but they did not realize it. To them the days were like any other; Jesus was no different from any other teacher.

Are you aware of how special *our day* is? Are you conscious of this special era in history in which you are living? Benefits and opportunities to recognize the living Christ abound as never before. We have the entire Bible, the guidance of the Spirit over more than two millennia of church history, and thousands of books explaining God's Word and doctrines. Millions around us desperately need to be evangelized. God is declaring to us: "Behold, *now* is the day of salvation, *now* is the accepted time." Are you aware of that, or are you oblivious to it? Be sure that such privileges and opportunities will not last forever. We may soon live through persecution when the rich treasures granted to us will no longer be available.

Second, *they had not responded to divine warnings:* "O Jerusalem, Jerusalem, thou that killest the prophets, and stonest them which are sent unto thee." For centuries, prophets had warned the people of Israel about God's justice and wrath against sin. Jesus Christ, the greatest Prophet of all, had spoken more plainly than every prophet before Him, and His warnings were more alarming. He said, "Be not afraid of them that kill the body, and after that have no more that they can do. But I will forewarn you whom ye shall fear: Fear him, which after he hath killed hath power to cast into hell; yea, I say unto you, Fear him" (Luke 12:4-5).

We, too, need to be more serious about the truth

of hell. Many people doubt that hell exists. But Jesus spoke constantly about hell—in fact, He spoke more about hell than all the Old Testament prophets combined. He was intensely aware of this place of eternal punishment. That is what made Him weep. Human beings can commit terrible brutality; we are reminded of that every day. Yet, without minimizing its awfulness, all human forms of brutality end. When we breathe our last, we are beyond the cruelty of other human beings, but death cannot bring us beyond the reach of God. Rather, we are *within* reach of the living God who is able to consign us, both soul and body, to hell. "Yea, I say to you," Jesus says, "Fear him."

We need to take God's warnings far more seriously than we do. We need to press them on our own consciences as well as others'. We need to be more honest and direct about God's judgment and wrath and the reality of hell. We don't need to be embarrassed by the doctrine of hell—you know that feeling.

After doing a funeral one day, I stopped at a restaurant to get a quick bite to eat. I stood in the back of a group of thirty people, debating whether I should wait or leave, when one of the employees, noticing my attire, said in a voice loud enough for everyone to hear: "Are you a minister?"

I replied, "Yes."

She said, "What church?"

"Heritage Reformed."

"Oh," she exclaimed, with increasing volume, "the *strict* church!"

"Well," I said, smiling now, but secretly hoping to deflect her: "We do try to be strictly scriptural."

She persisted: "Are you as strict as the Galatians?"

"Why don't you come and find out?" I said.

And then, the question came—even more loudly now: "Are you a *hell* and *damnation* preacher?"

Silence reigned. Everyone was listening. I almost wanted to say no. But I found myself saying rather meekly, "Come and see."

Later, I wish I had said, "I hope I am like my Savior, because He spoke more about hell than anyone else in the Bible, and He was honest with our souls."

Why was I embarrassed? Why are we embarrassed to take God's warnings seriously? Do we believe Him? Do we really believe in hell?

How many times have you heard serious warnings about the eternal, dreadful consequences of unbelief? How long have you been disregarding divine warnings? How often have you shrugged off this teaching, saying to yourself, "Oh well, that is how preachers are expected to preach. I do not need to take these things to heart. If the Lord will convert me, He'll convert me. For the rest, I'll live as I please. Besides, I'm not old yet; I'll take these things to heart later." Be careful! You do not know your day of "divine visitation"; your life may come to an end much sooner than you think.

Third, *they had ignored divine wooings.* Jesus

said, "How often would I have gathered thy children together, even as a hen gathereth her chickens under her wings, and ye would not!" The prophets had spoken tenderly to the people of Israel, trying to woo them back to the Lord, but the incarnate Son of God was even more persuasive. "Come unto me, all ye that labour and are heavy laden, and I will give you rest," He said. "Take my yoke upon you, and learn of me; for I am meek and lowly in heart: and ye shall find rest unto your souls. For my yoke is easy, and my burden is light" (Matt. 11:28-30).

How have you responded to Jesus' tender calls? How have you responded to His warnings? If you have been callous and indifferent to them, your "season of divine visitation" will soon end. You ought to think of God; you ought to think of Jesus Christ; you ought to come to Him simply because of who He is. But if you will not come to Him because of who He is, then think of your soul! Think of your eternity; think of the awfulness of hell. Today God shows you some measure of goodness and kindness, but He will not show you kindness in the unending, unbearable torments of hell. Of course you do not want to go to hell; but do you realize that hell is precisely where you are going if you spurn the invitations offered by the Messiah to find salvation in Him alone?

If only you knew, Jesus says, "the things that belong to your peace." Finding peace is more than not going to hell. Your peace lies in being forgiven, in being renewed in the image of God, in being blessed by Him, and in having eternal peace in heaven. If you will not think of *Him,* think of *yourself!*

If you will not think of Him or of yourself, then consider the tears of Jesus. He wept for those who would not weep for themselves, who did not think that they had anything to weep about. He mourned for those who were going down the broad road that leads to destruction; He wept for the perishing!

Jesus wept because God has no pleasure in the death of the wicked. He wept for hell-worthy, perishing sinners. The fault for your unbelief is yours; there is no one else in the entire world you can blame it on. But note this: though Jesus wept because of your willful unbelief, He did not excuse you from punishment. It is not by tears of repentance or by our prayers that atonement is made for our souls but only by the atoning blood of Jesus Christ. Because of Jesus' blood, "He is able to save to the uttermost all that come unto God by him" (Heb. 7:25). That includes you.

Do not neglect the time you have been given. Do not act like Jerusalem by ignoring the season of God's mercy and privileges. Jerusalem had a special season of mercy; God had provided for her salvation as for no other city. In Jerusalem, God set up His throne and provided His mercy seat and the brazen altar, dripping with substitutionary blood. To Jerusalem He sent prophets, priests, and kings to proclaim His way of messianic salvation; He sent John the Baptist, forerunner of the Messiah. And to Jerusalem

God sent the Messiah. She saw the greatest miracles ever performed and heard the most powerful preaching ever heard. The clearest calls to repentance were raised inside her walls. But Jerusalem did not honor the day of her visitation. She rejected the Messiah and cried for His death.

The matter is deep and mysterious, but according to Scripture, there are seasons in which nations, churches, and individuals are visited with special manifestations of God's presence—special seasons in which mercy is offered in a special manner. Eternity will reveal that the neglect of such manifestations and seasons was the turning point that led millions to eternal ruin. Though God had drawn very near to the people of Jerusalem and awakened their consciences, they rejected the Savior and trampled upon His blood and their own conscience.

Jesus wept over Jerusalem because her people refused to recognize the time of their visitation. The great Judgment Day is coming when impenitent Jerusalem and every impenitent sinner who has lived under the preaching of the gospel will cry out, "Mountains, fall on us; hills, cover us from the wrath of the Lamb!" Then the Judge-Lamb will pour out His wrath against all those who have not known the time of their visitation.

How are you responding to the times of divine visitation in your life—times when the gospel is freely offered, times when you become ill or are afflicted, times when the Holy Spirit is working in relatives and friends? Do you still fail to respond to God's tender wooings? Must Jesus Christ also weep because of your hardness of heart?

Have you ever wept tears over your own unbelief and hardness of heart? Have you ever wept tears out of love and longing for God? The Puritan Anthony Burgess said there should be twofold "mourning and weeping in our conversion to God": the mourning that accompanies the conviction of sin and the mourning that indicates longing for God. "Conversion is accompanied with a tearing or rending of the heart," Burgess says (*Spiritual Refining,* 1652, pp. 484-94).

Jesus was sinless, so He did not have to weep over His own sins, but dear believers, do you, like Jesus, weep tears of anguish for a world of unsaved sinners, a world lying in unrighteousness? Can you say with David: "Rivers of waters run down mine eyes, because they keep not thy law" (Ps. 119:136); with Jeremiah: "O that my head were waters, and mine eyes a fountain of tears, that I might weep day and night for the slain of the daughter of my people" (Jer. 9:1); and with Paul, "I have great heaviness and continual sorrow of heart...for my brethren" (Rom. 9:2-3)? Do you weep for your unsaved spouse, your unsaved children and relatives, your unsaved neighbors and work associates? Do you use all the means that God has placed within your reach to bring sinners to a saving interest in the work of Christ?

What do we weep over? If we each had two bot-

tles, and into one we put all the tears we shed for
ourselves in the past ten years and, into the other, all
the tears we have shed over lost souls, which bottle
would be fuller? Do most of our tears spring from
selfish, earthly concerns, or do they spring from concerns for the eternal souls of those around us? Have
we shed any tears we could claim before the Lord,
as David did: "Put thou my tears into thy bottle: are
they not in thy book?" (Ps. 56:8).

In the ancient world, especially in Persia and
Egypt, tears were often collected from the cheeks and
eyes of a mourner and stored in a bottle. That bottle
would be buried with the mourner to impress the
gods so they would be merciful to him. David wanted
his tears to be sanctified and preserved in God's bottle as confirmations of God's work which prompts
godly sorrow unto repentance "not to be repented of"
(2 Cor. 7:10). Tears motivated by godly sorrow are
precious to God because they reflect His own work
(2 Kings 20:4-5).

If we weep as Jesus weeps, we will consider every
unconverted person a mission field. We will weep
like John Welsh, the son-in-law of John Knox; Welsh
would get up in the middle of each night to pray for
the unsaved in his church. At times his wife would
call through the closed door of his prayer chamber,
"John, hadn't you better come back to bed?" His
usual answer was, "Oh, my dear wife, I have 3,000
souls to care for, and I know that many of them are
not yet right with God."

When David Brainerd wept over lost souls, he wrote: "Here am I, Lord, send me to the ends of the earth; send me to the rough, the savage pagans of the wilderness; send me from all that is called comfort in earth; send me even to death itself if it be but in Thy service and but to promote Thy kingdom." When Brainerd was very ill, he said, "Last year I longed to be prepared for the world of glory, and I desired speedily to depart out of this world, but of late all of my concern almost is for the conversion of the heathen, and to that end, I long to live."

John Paton, though he traveled all over the world, could not stop thinking about the people in the New Hebrides who did not know Christ. He said, "I continually heard the wail of the perishing heathen in the South Seas and I saw that few were caring for them."

We need a heart for God, for His mission, and for the souls of the lost. Being doctrinally sound is not enough. We need a flaming love for God and a weeping heart for the lost.

Parents, have you wept over the sinners in your own home? Do you give generously to foreign missions but have no burden for unsaved children in your home and in your neighborhood? Something is desperately wrong if you have no burden for missions, no burden for witnessing, no burden for lost souls.

What about you? How are you praying for evangelism and missionaries? Does your life resemble Andrew's, who brought his brother Simon to Jesus? Those who have truly found Christ ought to bring

others to Him. If God can save you and me, can He
not save anyone?

Jesus' Tears in Gethsemane

Hebrews 5:7 tells us that Jesus also wept in Gethsemane. It says that in the days of His flesh, Jesus
"offered up prayers and supplications with strong
crying and tears unto him that was able to save him
from death." The gospel writers do not specifically
record that Jesus wept in Gethsemane, but they
surely imply it in describing His agony even more
graphically than Hebrews does.

What kind of tears did Jesus shed in Gethsemane? Jesus did not weep out of self-pity, for that
would have excluded God from His thoughts. Christ's
tears in Gethsemane were tears of *godly fear*. While
He was weeping and praying, Jesus was address-
ing God in terms of tender love: "O my Father." He
concluded His prayer in tender submission, saying, "Not as I will, but as thou wilt" (Matt. 26:39).
He prayed with astonishing, unconditional, childlike
fear and obedience.

Jesus' tears were also of *sheer agony*. He prayed,
"If it be possible, let this cup pass from me" (Matt.
26:39). Jesus had experienced something of this
agony before. For example, in Luke 12:50, He had
said, "I have a baptism to be baptized with; and
how am I straitened"—literally, hemmed in, pressed
down—"till it be accomplished." Then, too, when
some Greeks came to the Feast of the Passover, Jesus

had a premonition of the consequence of His suffering and crucifixion. He spoke about a corn of wheat falling into the ground and dying, then said, "What shall I say? Father, save me from this hour. But for this cause came I unto this hour. Father, glorify thy name" (John 12:27-28). A shadow crossed His path on those two occasions, prompting Him to reveal some of the burden that was on Him. But never had He experienced agony like that in the Garden. This agony brought an "if" even to the lips of the Son of God, who willingly came to earth knowing what His Father wanted Him to do.

The shadow of suffering became real in Gethsemane, where Jesus' sufferings intensified. Matthew 26:37 says, "He began to be sorrowful and very heavy." As Jesus entered the Garden, a sorrow began to roll over Him that brought Him low in His mind and soul. He confessed, "My soul is exceeding sorrowful, even unto death" (Matt. 26:38).

Some commentators suggest that Hebrews 5:7 ("Unto him that was able to save him from death") means that Jesus was afraid that He would die in the Garden. I do not think it means that, but that interpretation comes close to what Jesus must have felt as He suffered in the Garden. He was brought so low in Himself that He felt like He was being stalked by death. He did not just get down on His knees to pray; He *sank* to His knees (Luke 22:41). Kneeling is a controlled action, but when we sink to our knees, we are under such pressure that we can no longer stand. An unseen hand pressed Jesus down.

Then that hand pressed harder until Jesus fell on His face on the ground (Matt. 26:39; Mark 14:35). He prayed the same prayer, the same words, three times. He prayed so hard that He sweated blood. There is a rare medical condition called hematibrosis, in which under the most intense agony, blood vessels erupt and blood seeps into sweat glands, breaking the surface of the skin. Apparently, Jesus went through something like this.

When Jesus wept in the Garden, He was in immense, imponderable agony. His human nature almost broke under the load. The tears were motivated not only by the fearsome suffering of crucifixion but by knowing that He would have to drink the cup of His Father's wrath, resist the temptation not to drink it to its bottom dregs, and submit to the powers of darkness. He would bear affliction that no other had borne because He would take on Himself the judgment and hell deserved by all His people.

Temptation was at hand. Satan was in the Garden, God was in the Garden, the God-man was in the Garden, and the cup was there. Jesus had to say "Thy will be done" in the most agonizing situation possible: the sinless One becoming sin, and bearing the full wrath of God! Jesus wept in inexpressible anguish.

We cannot possibly understand the depth of Jesus' suffering because we cannot understand how *rigorous God's justice* is and how *costly our salva-*

tion was. That God should so deal with His Son to bring Him to such agonizing tears—does this not tell us how awful sin is in the sight of God and how inflexible the Lord God is about the payment for sin? How dare any of us think that we can cope with God's justice apart from Christ! If that is what you think, my friends, consider this: If God did not spare His own sinless Son, on what grounds will He spare you and me, who are sinners? We have nothing in us that can justify us in His sight.

Jesus' tears also show us the great cost of our salvation. God did not save us by a divine wish. He saved us by the blood and agony of His Son, Jesus Christ. The Son of God had to take our sin upon Himself as if it were His own, even though His holy Being revolted against sin. He had to take our punishment as His own; He became sin and a curse for us. What kind of price can we put on that? The tears of the incarnate Son of God should move us to fear God's justice and love His salvation.

Our salvation has been paid for—not by Jesus' tears in the Garden of Gethsemane, but in spite of them. For Jesus went forward from Gethsemane in full obedience to God, knowing that He would give Himself as *the* sacrifice to God for our sins. Do not weep for Him; rather, let us weep for ourselves and our children for whom this sacrifice was necessary because of our sin.

We can never weep such tears as Jesus did in the Garden. We cannot possibly comprehend the depth

of that sorrow. Jesus mercifully wept those tears
for us that we might not have to weep in hell forever. And yet, Jesus' tears should move us to tears in
three ways:

First, our tears should be motivated by *godly fear*.
As believers en route to "a better country," we must
pass through our own Garden of Sorrows, where we
learn that "the disciple is not above his master, nor
the servant above his lord" (Matt. 10:24). Trials must
come, and by the grace of the Spirit, they will move
us to godly fear so that we learn to cry out as we are
given the cup of suffering, "nevertheless, not as I will,
but as thou wilt" (Matt. 26:39). Pray for much grace
to bear the tearful anguish of your own Gethsemanes
in unmurmuring submission.

Second, our tears must be motivated by *divine
love*. Have you ever wept over the staggering love
of the Father in asking His Son to bear such agony
as the cross, and the staggering love of the Son to
endure it?

Several years ago, I was accosted by some men in
Latvia after an evening of teaching. They bound my
face, hands, and feet, then ran a knife up and down
my spine, and periodically slapped my face with it,
shouting, "Mafia! Mafia!" For forty-five minutes, I
felt sure I was going to die. During that time, however, I felt wonderfully sustained by one thing—the
blood of Jesus. Meditating on His substitutionary
blood gave me unspeakable calm and peace. All that
mattered was that I was washed in His blood. I felt

more like weeping over the stupendous love of the
Father in giving His Son to the bloody cross than I
did about my own impending death.

Dear friend, you need that blood, the blood of
Christ's salvation and love. Daniel Smart, a nine-
teenth century Baptist preacher, once remarked, "The
sweetest tears a believer sheds are always in relation
to the precious blood of Jesus Christ."

Third, our tears must be motivated by *redemption's price.* Have you looked at Jesus, whom your sins
have pierced, and mourned for Him, overwhelmed
by the price He paid to secure your salvation (Zech.
12:10)? Have you wept over sin because of what it
has cost our blessed Immanuel? Oh, how we trivialize sin! Dear friends, if your soul enters Gethsemane
even for one night, you will never be able to speak
lightly of sin again.

I've had the privilege of visiting the Garden of
Gethsemane on two occasions. Once, I had several
minutes alone under one of the ancient olive trees in
Gethsemane. They were the most sacred moments of
my time in Israel. I meditated on my Savior crawling
on the ground there, weeping, agonizing, asking if
the cup might pass. Thank God the cup could not
pass! Thank God He had to drink it to its bottom
bitter dregs for me—every drop, for me. Mary Winslow once wrote, "If I were the only sinner for which
He ever had to die, His sufferings would have been
just as exhaustive as they were, given the enormity
of my sin."

Sin is heinous. There are no words to describe the dreadful nature of sin any more than there are words that can describe the nature of Jesus' tears in Gethsemane.

Jesus wept tears of tender sympathy and of groaning anger at Bethany; He wept tears of anguish and lamentation at Jerusalem; He wept tears of godly fear and sheer agony at Gethsemane. All of His tears were shed in light of our sin, dear children of God. Will you not admire His grace with awe?

That He should leave His place on high,
And come for sinful man, to die;
It is a thing most wonderful,
Almost too wonderful to be,
That God's own Son should come from heaven,
And die to save a child like me.

Dear friends, what kind of tears do you shed? Do you walk as Jesus walked, weeping as He wept? Do you weep for those walking deep in sin without a care for salvation? Do you weep out of hatred for sin? Do you weep because of the amazing love of God in Christ revealed to us in the gospel? Do you weep in the footsteps of Christ as you look forward to that day when God will wipe away all your tears (Rev. 21:4)?

If so, you will emerge from the Garden of Tears one day into the radiance of the heavenly Eden. You will be seated on the throne that Christ gives you and bask in the sunshine of His favor. You will enjoy His endless friendship through a tearless eternity. You will experience what Gerald Massey suggested when he wrote:

> *The sap is bitter in the bark,*
> *That sweetens in the fruit above;*
> *And spirits toiling through the dark,*
> *Shall reach at last their light of love.*

Dear friend, if you do not know the precious, weeping Christ as your own Savior, will you not bow before Him now? He is a Savior full of anger against sin, but full of compassion toward our plight and full of power to execute our redemption. He can save you—today.

I read recently of a Scottish Highland shepherd boy who was sheltering his sheep in a cave one evening because of a ferocious storm. The next morning, to his horror, he noticed that the central viaduct of an extensive bridge that stretched across a wide gulf was washed away by the storm. The shepherd boy knew that a train was coming soon. In a flash, he scrambled up the embankment, and tore his way through the bushes. Bruised and breathless, he reached the track just in time to wave down the train. The conductor, however, waved him away. The boy fell onto the tracks. The conductor hit the brakes just in time; the train stopped at the edge of the abyss. The people on the train awoke and were soon led by the conductor to see the mangled body of the shepherd boy who died for them.

Dear friend, if Jesus had not wept, suffered, and died for sinners, if He had not come to lay across the track of our lives and to call to us, *"Come unto me all you that are weary and heavy laden,"* you and I would end in the eternal abyss.

Why do you keep trying to wave away Jesus' loving warnings? Why do you reject the gospel? Will you rush over the dead body of Jesus again today, and once more deny Him as the resurrected and living Lord? Cast all your sins upon Him, believe in Him, surrender to Him as Lord; you will never regret it. And you will know tears of joy and tears of sorrow as you have never known before.

4

Jesus' Endurance and Ours

"Never, never, never give up!" That was the essence of one of Winston Churchill's commencement addresses. The message was: "Keep on keeping on." Never giving up is a tough assignment when it comes to walking as Jesus walked in areas such as cross-bearing, office-bearing, and weeping. How do we persevere in such ways?

It is one thing to begin the Christian life and quite another to persevere in it. It is one thing to repent and believe the gospel and quite another to go on repenting and believing. The miracle of Pentecost in Acts 2:4 is remarkable, but, in some ways, Acts 2:42 is even more remarkable: "And they continued stead-fastly in the apostles' doctrine and fellowship and in breaking of bread, and in prayers." My father often said to me: "Remember, it's relatively easy to begin a ministry in the church; the challenge is to maintain it—to persevere in zeal for it."

Have you, too, discovered that it can be harder to go on believing as a Christian than to become one in the first place? Do you find that enduring can be an enormous challenge?

Perhaps even now you are fearful. "This conference is a great boost for my faith," you say. "The Christ-centered exposition of the Scriptures energizes me. And I love the spiritual fellowship. But I know myself all too well. Within a week or two, I am afraid I will fall back into my old routine of living as a mediocre Christian, lacking zeal to walk as Christ walked. I am afraid I will fall back into defeat and say, 'I can never measure up to walking as Jesus walked, so what's the use of trying? The poverty of my ongoing faith and sanctification is terribly discouraging. How can I persevere in believing in the absence of anything tangible to confirm my faith? How can I go on believing that God is light in the darkest night? How can I persevere in paying the high cost of faithfulness, enduring persecution, affliction, and loss for the gospel's sake?'"

Every Christian faces numerous discouragements while striving to walk as Christ walked. Our hands hang down when we face personal failure, when others let us down, or when providence frustrates our desires. Disappointment promotes discouragement, and discouragement brings us to our knees. We feel weak and tired, emotionally and spiritually, and are tempted to give up. What's the use of continuing to fight temptation when everything seems to work against us? What's the use of persevering and enduring when everything seems hopeless? We say with Asaph, "Verily I have cleansed my heart in vain" (Ps. 73:13).

So how do we endure in the Christian race when the motivation to press on fades and our life of holiness weakens, when we are in danger of giving up the fight against our besetting sin, and when it seems that God is not answering our prayers?

The answer is profound yet simple: We endure as Christ endured when He was tempted to surrender in the battle of spiritual warfare. We walk as He walked, by His grace and His strength.

Hebrews 12 teaches us how Christ endured. Let us focus on verses 1-3: "Wherefore seeing we also are compassed about with so great a cloud of witnesses, let us lay aside every weight, and the sin which doth so easily beset us, and let us run with patience the race that is set before us, looking unto Jesus the author and finisher of our faith; who for the joy that was set before him endured the cross, despising the shame, and is set down at the right hand of the throne of God. For consider him that endured such contradiction of sinners against himself, lest ye be wearied and faint in your minds."

Let us explore the subject of Jesus' Endurance and Ours from three aspects: (1) its mission, (2) its manner, and (3) its motives.

The Mission

The author of Hebrews ministered to the Jewish Christians around 68 A.D., shortly before the Romans

destroyed Jerusalem and its temple. The book was
written like a sermon to encourage discouraged Jewish converts who were paying too much attention to
Christ-rejecting Jews. These unbelieving Jews were
challenging the spiritual worship that the Jewish
Christians enjoyed in Jesus Christ. Many were saying, "Where is your temple, where are your high
priests?" Some were persecuting Jewish believers
by marginalizing them socially. Others were persecuting believers more openly, withholding jobs and
other benefits from them. As a result, many Jewish Christians suffered "reproaches and afflictions"
(Heb. 10:32-34), and were discouraged and tempted
to abandon the faith.

The author of Hebrews encourages these Christian Jews by explaining how all the Old Testament
rituals and ceremonial laws have been fulfilled in
the Lord Jesus Christ. In the first nine chapters, the
writer points believers to Christ, the greatest High
Priest who brought a perfect sacrifice and who makes
perfect intercession. Chapters 10-13 then focus on
how we are to live out of Christ's saving work, freely
approaching God's throne of grace. These chapters
answer poignant questions: What's the use of going
on? Why should we endure in the Christian faith?
What consequences does Christ's work have for the
lives of believers?

Our world today is surprisingly like that of the
Christian Hebrews. Many leaders in the religious
world look down on conservative evangelicals and

regard us as a kind of modern day "Puritan killjoy." Like the Christian Hebrews, we often feel rejected, marginalized, even ostracized and persecuted.

You know what I mean, young people. Some of you are not in the "in" group at school or work because of your faith. You're considered goody-goodies. You're out of touch, rejected from the inner circle, teased, perhaps. It's tempting at times to ask: "How can I keep going?"

The Christian Hebrews' need for endurance is evident not only from our text, but also from several other chapters in Hebrews. Actually, there are ninety-six verses in Hebrews that encourage Christians to endure in faith. For example, Hebrews 10:23 says, "Let us hold fast the profession of our faith without wavering." And 10:36 says, "For ye have need of patience, that after ye have done the will of God, ye might receive the promise." Chapter 11 offers powerful examples of Old Testament stalwarts who endured spiritually "by faith." These heroes show us the virtue and power of faith.

Chapter 12 goes on to say: "Wherefore seeing we also are compassed about with so great a cloud of witnesses, let us lay aside every weight, and the sin which doth so easily beset us, and let us run with patience the race that is set before us." The Greek word here translated as *patience* is identical with the word used in verses 2 and 3, translated as *endurance*. So each of the first three verses in Hebrews 12 uses the word *endurance*. Verse 1 teaches us, "We need to run the race with endurance"; verse 2 informs us that Jesus "endured the cross"; and verse 3 claims that Jesus "endured contradiction." *Endurance* is the best translation in this context, since the author obviously wants to emphasize that this patience is an active Christian grace; it doesn't just sit and wait. Endurance involves hard labor and implies faithfully carrying a burden. The emphasis in verse 1 is on the last part of the verse: "Let us run with patience [or with endurance] the race that is set before us."

Thus our mission of endurance is to *run our Christian race to its end "with patience."* Using the metaphor of a race, the writer has in mind the endurance-testing relay races that took place in great coliseums. Those races didn't focus on who were the fastest sprinters, but on which runners would reach the finish line. Relay races were distance events. The contestants in the Christian race include the author of Hebrews, the Hebrew Christians to whom he writes, and, by mutual faith, *us*. Ultimately, every Christian is in the race. The Christian life is a test in endurance, a long relay in which runners assist each other rather than compete against each other. It's a serious race, a race that involves the testing and taxing of our faith, strength, and character. Life and death are set before us; hence, we must persevere. We must keep on keeping on. We cannot just step out of this race when we tire; we have to run all the way to the finish line.

This race of endurance is to be run "with

patience," we are told. The Christian race has to be run steadily, deliberately, and actively every day, making use of the means of grace—reading and searching the Scriptures, personal and intercessory prayer, reading sound literature, fellowship among the saints, and Sabbath-keeping. The Christian life is not passive; we must work out our own salvation with fear and trembling, knowing that it is God who works in us both to will and to do of His good pleasure (Phil. 2:12-13).

We believe in both the preservation of the saints by God and the perseverance of the saints before God. True, our perseverance is a fruit of God's preservation, but that perseverance is still ours. It doesn't happen objectively outside of us; it happens subjectively, by grace, within and through us. So we must persevere. We must run the race. We cannot remain on the sidelines; we are not mere spectators.

We must continue the race patiently, stedfastly, believing in the Lord—not only in times of prosperity, but also in times of adversity (cf. Phil. 3:13-14). Regardless of circumstance, we must put our trust in the Lord every day. Our challenge is to stay focused on the Lord while we live in the midst of trials (cf. Ps. 46). The word translated as *endured* means to *stay* or to *press on*, even when the burden becomes too heavy. When we carry a burden that becomes too heavy, we want to rest for a while. But the apostle says that we need to "press on" by faith. That is what endurance is all about—to keep hoping and trusting in the Lord, even when everything seems to go against us. It means to say with Job, "Though he slay me, yet will I trust in him" (Job 13:15)—that is, to trust in God as my greatest Friend when He seems to be acting as if He were my greatest Enemy. It is easy to trust in the Lord when everything is going well, but how hard it becomes when much in our lives seems to testify against us! How easily our faith weakens and our diligent use of the means of grace is thwarted in times of difficulty!

Those who shall one day enter into glory must face numerous trials here on earth. Revelation 7:14 says that those who enter into heaven come "out of great tribulation." The believer has some foretaste of heavenly glory on earth, but this earth is not heaven for him. Here on earth, we do not yet enjoy the full salvation promised to believers. We have not yet received the full measure of God's grace. Here on earth our mission is to endure, to be patient runners in the Christian race. But how do we do that?

The Manner
We are to run the Christian race, says our text, with both a negative and a positive perspective. Negatively, we must rid ourselves of sin and hindrances. "Let us lay aside every weight [that is, every hindrance], and the sin which doth so easily beset us [that is, not just our besetting or 'favorite' sin, but all sin], and [so] let us run with patience the race that is set before us" (Heb. 12:1).

The apostle is speaking particularly here to Christians. To run the race and reach the finish line, he tells them, they must not be hindered by anything; they must "lay aside every weight." How foolish a runner would be to wear heavy clothing and carry all kinds of paraphernalia while running a race! Like Greek athletes who trained naked or with a minimal amount of clothing, a runner who wants to reach the finish line needs to get rid of everything that hinders him.

And so it is with believers. The race we run is difficult and the battle severe. We need much endurance because there is much that hinders us and stands in our way. Unbelief, fear, worry, love of things, cares of this life, and even legitimate things such as relationships, professional duties, and recreational pursuits, when given an undue proportion of our time and heart, can hinder us in our Christian race.

So it is critical to discard anything that hinders us in this race. As a young man, I had to give up playing basketball for my high school team because of the time it consumed and the pride it engendered. Stuart Olyott says, "For some of you this will mean canceling your subscription to the Internet, getting rid of your TV or stopping reading certain sorts of books or magazines. For others it will mean giving up football or a favorite sport, or even ending unhelpful friendships. We are all vulnerable, but we are not all vulnerable in the same areas" *(The Way to Godliness,* p. 28).

Sin is our great enemy in the Christian race. The

words, "the sin which doth so easily beset us," can be translated as the sin that *entangles* us, that trips us up. Sin compasses us about; it clings to us. It comes out onto the racetrack, hangs onto our neck, and clings to us like clothing. "Sin," as John Owen put it, "is always at our elbow."

Sin takes our eyes off of our Savior; it interrupts our relationship with God. Sin is anti-God. It makes us worldly, selfish, proud, and unbelieving. Sin is spiritual insanity. Is that how you regard sin?

There is a difference, of course, in how unbelievers and believers regard sin: unbelievers cling to sin, while sin clings to believers. That is to say, unbelievers reach out for sin. They delight in it, look for it, and embrace it. But believers despise and hate sin. They try to stay free from sin and break loose from it, but discover to their dismay that sin clings to them.

To put off sin and all other hindrances is not easy. We can't just put them off as we would take off a coat. And yet, we must do it. We must deny whatever hinders us in the Christian race and use all the means of grace to help us in our race. That is what runners do today. They deny themselves anything that would hinder them. They eat the right foods and get the right exercise. They do anything that will help them run and avoid anything that will distract their minds. If athletes are that serious about running an earthly race, how serious should we be about running the heavenly race?

Perhaps you find this extremely difficult to do. It

is, but God never said that the Christian race would be easy. We must realize that we are accountable for what we do and don't do in our race. We must understand that we are not victims of sin; hindrances do not just overcome us. The imperative to lay aside every weight implies that we are responsible for those weights and the sin that still besets us so easily. We must put off the conversation and activities of our old nature and put on the righteousness and holiness of the new man (Eph. 4:22–24). There is simply no other way to run this race.

To run the Christian race with endurance means doing continual battle against every weight and every sin. We must become increasingly conscious of them; every day, we must decide against them, say no to them, and put them to death. We cannot trivialize sin, dumb it down, desensitize our consciences, or let down our guard. We cannot just let sin happen; we cannot let it penetrate our souls and our lives.

As the Puritans would say, we must not let sin into the gates of our soul through our senses; we must guard eye-gate and ear-gate. And when we do open the gates too wide to sin and stumble, we must confess and forsake our sin, immediately. We must put a sword through sin; we must push it back out the gates of our soul and close the gates. We must fear and hate sin. We must realize that it entangles us and hinders our walk with the Lord.

Sometimes we may be tempted to give up this battle against sin. "What's the use?" we ask. We have fought sin again and again, yet we keep stumbling and falling into it. We fear that we have become nothing but sin, and there is no point in staying in the race. But that reasoning is unbiblical, false, and satanic, dear believer. Thanks be to God, sin can be laid aside. Sin does not belong to you as a believer; it does not belong to your new nature. It clings to you, but it is not you. In Romans 6:11, Paul tells us to "reckon yourselves to be dead indeed unto sin, but alive unto God through Jesus Christ our Lord." Sin is not your life—*Christ* is! Sin is a thievish, foreign intruder; you must not let it rest in the home of your new heart. You may not accept it as part of you. An old, now-deceased elder in my congregation used to say, "My father always told us: as a Christian, you have no business sinning."

An elderly Welsh woman once told me that when two men broke into her home and tied her up, she said to them, "You young men have no right to intrude into my home and steal my possessions." She told them that they would have to give an account to God on the Judgment Day for what they were doing this very moment. Eventually, her words were too much for their consciences and they left.

That's how we should confront ourselves when sin intrudes with its ugly, thievish character into our souls. We ought to remind ourselves that sin will return on the Judgment Day and, in the name of our Savior and on the basis of His Word, tell sin to be gone.

How do you view sin and other hindrances? Do

you welcome and tolerate sin, or do you fight it and flee from it? Do you fatalistically resign yourself to other, seemingly lawful hindrances, or do you conscientiously lay them aside?

John Bunyan once said that if sin knocks on your door and you open the door, you have not sinned as long as you shut the door as soon as you recognize sin for what it is. We fall into sin when we welcome sin into the home of our minds and dwell upon it.

Perhaps you respond, "I see my need for endurance in the Christian race, and I understand that endurance means laying aside sin and various hindrances, but how do I do that?"

You do that by adopting a positive perspective: by looking to Jesus, by confessing Him, and by appropriating forgiveness and learning to live by faith as a forgiven sinner throughout the Christian race. As Hebrews 12:2 says, "Let us run with patience the race that is set before us, looking unto Jesus the author and finisher of our faith." To persevere in the Christian race, we need to look beyond the weights of sin that surround us. We need to look to Jesus who ran before us and endured perfectly.

The context of our verses make plain that to run the Christian race, we need to focus by *faith* on Jesus, in whom we find strength, and who is both our model runner and our coach. Just as the Old Testament saints lived by faith in the promises of God (Heb. 11), so we, surrounded by them as a cloud of witnesses, must focus by faith on Jesus alone, in whom all the promises of God "are yea and amen." Enduring is a matter of faith, and this faith depends on Jesus Christ.

The apostle reminds us in verses 2 and 3 that Jesus' endurance and ours are intimately connected. Jesus is called here "the author and finisher of our faith." How can we be sure that our faith is not in vain—that we will actually complete this race by faith? We can be sure because of Jesus, our uniquely qualified supplier and sustainer of faith, who evokes and stimulates our faith. Jesus is the pioneer and perfecter of our salvation (Heb. 2:10; 4:14-16). He will not allow a single one of His children to fall to the side of the road because He is the finisher of the faith of His runners. Because faith is the gift and work of Jesus Christ from its origin to its completion, our faith will never be in vain and we will never appeal to Christ in vain. Therefore, our faith must be directed to and concentrated on Christ, the only Mediator. He is the supreme exponent of faith.

The Motives
Speaking on behalf of Christ, the author of our text in Hebrews acts like a coach giving a motivational talk to his runners before a big race. We need such talks! There are three parts to his talk: the first and primary motivation for running the race of life is *the example of Christ*. We need to look to Him, "who for the joy that was set before him endured the cross, despising the shame and is set down at the right hand of the

throne of God" (v. 2). Our Savior motivates us to run this race in three important ways.

The example of Christ

First, we are motivated by *what He endured*. Jesus Christ, the holy Lamb of God, Creator of this world, "endured the cross"! The cross comprehends the worst punishment Jesus could receive in this world. He suffered throughout all of His earthly life, but the cross was the ultimate suffering. Jesus was nailed to it as the chief of sinners; He bore the punishment of His Father for the sins of His elect; He endured being forsaken by His Father, whom He loved from all eternity.

Jesus Christ hung in the naked flame of His Father's wrath for six long hours on the cross. No eye of mercy was cast toward Him, implying, "We understand." Seemingly rejected by heaven, earth, and hell, He endured the cross until its bitter end. No words can begin to capture the extremity of His sufferings, when He cried out, "My God, my God, why hast thou forsaken me?" (Matt. 27:46). At the cross, He descended into the essence of what hell is; it was the most climactic moment of suffering ever endured, an hour so compacted—so infinite—so horrendous—as to be seemingly unsustainable.

Though we cannot grasp the depth of what this forsakenness was for Jesus, we know that it was far more awful that we can imagine. This forsakenness appears to have included some temporary loss of the

sense of His sonship, some loss of filial conscious-
ness. In Gethsemane, and in the first and last words
of the cross, Jesus was able to call on God as His
Father. But at the height of His dereliction on the
cross, His cry was "Eloi, Eloi." He was aware of the
goodness of God, the otherness of God, the power
and holiness of God, and even that that God was His
God as God, but He lost in some degree His sense of
sonship in that dread moment. He knew more of sin-
nership than sonship at that solemn moment. He felt
your and my sin, dear believer. In His self-image, He
was not the Beloved in whom God was well-pleased,
but the cursed one; vile, foul, repulsive—an object of
dread. This is the essence of the dereliction. This is
what God thinks of sin; the price of what Christ, the
God-man, had to pay for sin.

Jesus endured the cross even when He was aban-
doned by God. As the Eternal Word, Jesus had always
been with God; as the incarnate Son, He had always
been with the Father. Father and Son had gone up
from Bethlehem to Calvary together, like Abraham and Isaac going up the mount in Genesis 22.
But now, in the hour of Christ's greatest need, God
was not there. When the Son most needed encouragement, no voice cried from heaven, "This is my
beloved son." When He most needed reassurance, no
one said, "I am well pleased." No grace was extended
to Him, no favor shown, no comfort administered,
no part of the cup removed. God was present only
as one displeased, as one bearing down upon Christ

with profound wrath. Every detail declares the irrationality, the heinousness, the dread character of sin. And yet, Christ endured the cross!

Jesus endured the cross, our text says, "for the joy that was set before him." This word *for* can also mean *instead of.* From that perspective, the Lord Jesus did not endure the cross to gain joy for Himself. With His Father and the Spirit, He already possessed that joy from all eternity. Certainly He was motivated by love to impart eternal joy for sinners, but our text emphasizes that Jesus endured the cross while He was already partaker of the heavenly joy with His Father and the Holy Spirit.

So the cross was not only a way *to* glory; it was also a way *from* glory. The Lord Jesus Christ was willing to leave the joy that He already enjoyed to travel the Via Dolorosa. The Lamb of God suffered for thirty-three years on this earth, culminating in His suffering on the cross. Four short words—"Jesus endured the cross"—summarize all of Christ's love and willingness to suffer for sinners. He deserved a crown, but He willingly endured a cross. He did not deserve to dirty His feet with this world's dust, yet He was willing to have them nailed to Calvary's cross. Actively and consciously, He remained faithful to the work the Father laid upon His shoulders. He did not waver, He did not hesitate; He endured.

At one point, Jesus stumbled under the weight of the cross, and Simon had to carry it for Him. But help along the way didn't mean that the cross was less of a punishment for Christ. It only meant that He was meant to die on the cross rather than on the roadside. Our dear Lord Jesus Christ endured every hour, every minute, every second on the cross. We know that when we have much pain, time seems to slow down. Hours creep by. So it was for Jesus. In all His agony and pain, He accepted every second of pain. His every breath embraced the cross.

We too must endure in our race, but we do not have to endure the cross like Jesus Christ had to do. His huge crosses make all our crosses small! He endured things more fearful and overwhelming than we will ever have to face. He endured the cross to merit our salvation; we endure our crosses out of gratitude for the gift of His salvation. Nevertheless, Jesus' attitude of being willing to forego joy for the sake of submissive cross-bearing is an attitude that we must cultivate. Daily, we must pray for willingness to bear every cross He deems fit to place upon us. We must endure because He endured, to persevere because He persevered. We are called to endure right now, in the midst of our personal struggles. We are called to pause, to stand in awe, and to watch the Lord Jesus Christ. We are called to look to Jesus and consider how He suffered and died. We can become so accustomed to failure in our battles with sin and so busy attempting to sanctify ourselves in our own strength that we fail to meditate on the suffering of the Lord Jesus Christ. If we fail to focus on

Christ, we will lack the mercy and grace we need to run the race.

Second, we are motivated by *what He rejoiced in*. The phrase *for the joy* is rooted in Jesus' exalted state of glory, where He "is set down at the right hand of the throne of God." The cross was not Jesus' end point. He rejoiced under the cross, knowing that He would be the victor in the battle with the powers of evil, and that He would soon be resurrected by His Father and taken home to glory to receive His promised reward. The joy that was set before Him was the joy of His own homecoming, the joy of reunion with His Father, the joy of being crowned with honor and glory and having all things put under His feet (Heb. 2:6-8). It was the joy of bringing many sons to glory (2:10). Jesus rejoiced, knowing that He would gain more than He lost.

Dear believer, as Christ lived out this joy with certitude, so we are to joyously await the eternal weight of glory, knowing that our future home with Christ in heaven is secure. We rejoice by faith (Heb. 11:1), knowing that our eyes have not seen, nor have our ears heard, nor has it entered into our hearts, what God has prepared for those who love Him (1 Cor. 2:9). Our future is to be married to Christ forever! That sure hope of glory and gracious reward in Christ ought to motivate us to run the Christian race.

Third, we are motivated by *what He despised*. Many of us have perhaps thought, "What a shame! Jesus, the Son of God, on the cross!" And yet the Son of God thought little of the shame the cross brought upon Him. When our first parents, Adam and Eve, fell in Paradise, they felt shame because of their sin. This shame Jesus now bore on the cross, where He was made shameful sin. That shame was more intense than His pain. But He despised that shame and willingly endured the cross. He did not grumble or protest. He did not ask for a retrial because of the punishment and sentence of the cross. He endured the cross, "despising the shame."

Dear friends, when others mock us for running the Christian race, despise the shame. Be like Christian in *Pilgrim's Progress,* who began the race by shouting, "Life, life, eternal life," even as his family and friends called to him to come back. Let Christ be your mentor. Live by the fear of God, not the fear of man, "esteeming the smiles and frowns of God to be of greater weight and value than the smiles and frowns of men," as John Brown put it. Despise the world's shame. Count it all joy when you suffer for Christ's sake. Let Christ's willingness to endure shame motivate you to endure.

The witness of the saints

A second important motive that encourages us to endure in the Christian race is *the witness of the saints.* Even as we are surrounded with sin and various impediments while we run the Christian race, we are also surrounded with people in the stands who encourage us to endure. Verse 1 says, "Wherefore seeing we also are compassed about with so great a cloud of witnesses." These Old Testament heroes of faith encourage us in three ways. First, they encourage us because they were faithful spiritual athletes in the past. Every one of them was a gold medal winner in the race of life. Their example of running bears witness to enduring faith, so that, like Abel, they "being dead, yet speak" (Heb. 11:4) to us, encouraging us to run.

Second, because they reached the finish line by the endurance of faith, they cheer us on to persevere by putting our faith in God and the Messiah, just as they have done. These witnesses declare to us from the Old Testament pages that the Lord is faithful and willing through His Son to help us, too, despite all our stumblings, to endure to the end of the race.

How great a motivation these Old Testament witnesses are! What motivation Enoch provided in that "he pleased God" (Heb. 11:5-6)! What motivation Abraham offered by obeying God in following His will to an unknown place, living "in the land of promise, as in a strange country" (vv. 8-9)! What motivation Joseph provided when he gave "commandment concerning his bones" (v. 22)! What motivation Moses presented when he chose rather "to suffer affliction with the people of God, than to enjoy the pleasures of sin for a season, esteeming the reproach of Christ greater riches than the treasures in Egypt" (vv. 25-26). Those Old Testament saints who lived by faith surround us, Hebrews 11 and 12 say, like a crowd of

spectators, watching us endure, nodding in encouragement, and saying, "If I, by grace, endured to the
end, so can you."

As we read the Old Testament, we surround ourselves with saints who have lived by faith. They show
us that the Lord is faithful to His own, even in the
midst of trials that far supersede our own. Hebrews
11:37 says, "They were stoned, they were sawn
asunder, were tempted, were slain with the sword:
they wandered about in sheepskins and goatskins;
being destitute, afflicted, tormented." And yet they
endured by faith, clinging to God and His promises
(v. 39). The Lord surrounds us with these kinds of
people. Now, if they have run the difficult race set
before them with patience and with endurance, how
much more should we? If they did not give up in the
face of insurmountable odds, why should we? If the
Lord graciously brought these saints to the finish
line, why couldn't He also bring us there—we who
have so few discouragements and crosses to bear
compared to them?

This cloud of witnesses increases in number
throughout the New Testament and church history,
with people such as Paul and John, as well as Athana-
sius, Augustine, Luther, Calvin, Whitefield, Spurgeon,
Lloyd-Jones—who pressed forward through life by
faith despite formidable obstacles and opposition.
What encouragement these Bible saints and great
divines throughout the ages are for us today!

Luther was so encouraged by the Psalms when

he was going through his own trials that he said, "I can scarcely see how you can be a Christian without David being one of your best friends." And as he read the divines of past generations, Luther quipped: "Some of my best friends are dead ones." Can you not say the same thing? What encouragement is found in David, Isaiah, Paul, John, Calvin, William Perkins, Wilhelmus à Brakel, Thomas Goodwin, John Owen, Anthony Burgess, John Bunyan, Samuel Rutherford, Mary Winslow, Ruth Bryan, and J.C. Ryle! Praise be to God for this cloud of witnesses who have encouraged us by their lives and writings to endure by gracious faith. Sometimes they have so moved me by the love of Christ or so challenged me by their godliness or so instructed me by their spiritual insights that I scarcely know where I would be without this cloud of God's witnesses. I do not doubt you know what I am talking about.

This cloud of witnesses encourages us to think realistically about the communion of saints (*communio sanctorum)*. Could it be that the saints in glory are more deeply interested in how we run the Christian race than we realize and are closer to us than we may think? Certainly, we err in taking little interest in those who have gone before us, for we have much to learn from them about running this great race. They are teammates who have reached the goal, but they will not be crowned until we join their ranks and share in their victory. They are eagerly waiting for that day, and urge us onward and forward by their own examples of endurance. We need to endure because of the cloud of witnesses that surrounds us.

Third, living witnesses still surround us today. There are live people in the stands watching us and encouraging us to run the race. My witnesses include my God-fearing wife, my God-fearing friends in my church, and dear children of God around the world—yes, even many of you in this large hall today. Some of you love this conference and come back year after year because you, too, want to be surrounded, encouraged, directed, and challenged by a living cloud of witnesses. We believe in the communion of saints and in maintaining fellowship among believers. God's people were never meant to be lone rangers; we need fellowship with each other. The beginners in faith need the mature in faith for guidance; the mature need the beginners for renewed enthusiasm. We need to speak with each other about the faithfulness of our Savior and the ways of God so that we can encourage each other to be faithful in running the race.

Perhaps you are a widow or widower. It has been years since your spouse passed away. You have church friends, but those long evenings are hard to endure. You feel so alone at times. Take heart; the verse here says that you are surrounded by a great cloud of spectators watching you to encourage you in this struggle. Will you remain faithful? Be encouraged, you are not alone; you belong to a large family.

Recently, a young woman came up to me in tears

after I spoke at a conference, saying, "I am an orphan and an only child. I have only one uncle, who lives on the other side of the world. Lately, I have been weeping myself to sleep because of loneliness. But today, you helped me see that I am part of a big family. God is my Father, Jesus is my older Brother, all the believers in this church are my brothers and sisters. Now I have a new take on life and have courage to go on!"

Some people in this cloud of witnesses encourage us in special ways. They may not be famous and important in the eyes of others, but they are very important to us. For me, Samuel Rutherford is a great witness. His *Letters,* which lie on the night stand beside my bed, have encouraged me countless times when I felt weighed down by affliction. If Rutherford can see afflictions as signs of Jesus coming, why shouldn't I?

I think also of my father, who often said to me before he died, "Preach Christ in the simplicity of the gospel. You can never preach Him too much!" Or my dear wife, who notices even on the way to church when I feel harassed by Satan and fear I can't preach. "You have it again, don't you?" she asks. "It will be alright; your Savior won't desert you; He'll help you once more." Oh, how such witnesses encourage me to endure, to strive more diligently, to be more godly! Persevere, dear friends, on account of the cloud of witnesses that compass you about.

Strength and peace of mind

Finally, be motivated to endure like Christ for your
own strength and peace of mind. Hebrews 12:3 says,
"For consider him that endured such contradiction
of sinners against himself, lest ye be wearied and
faint in your minds." This refers back to verse 2,
telling us how Jesus endured the cross. It says that
Jesus endured "such contradiction," that is, all the
hatred, opposition, gainsaying, and contempt of sinners against Himself. The word *contradiction* here
is the same word used in the Septuagint, the Greek
translation of the Old Testament, when the rebellious Israelites argued with Moses. In the midst of
such rebels—priests, scribes, and soldiers who spoke
out against Him—Jesus had to suffer.

Jesus endured such contradiction of sinners
because of His great love for them. We are moved
when someone surrenders his life for a friend, but
Jesus gave His life for enemies (Rom. 5:10) such
as you and me, who are prone to talk back to God
and to argue about His ways. By nature, we do not
surrender and receive what He has done, but rebel
against it; but when God penetrates our hearts with
His saving grace, we are made willing to receive His
gospel grace. We, too, will have to suffer contradiction and hostility from those around us, for all who
are in Christ Jesus will suffer persecution. We will
never endure the magnitude of Christ's contradiction
of sinners, but if we walk as He walked, we will cer-

tainly encounter the contradiction of sinners against us. But all of this has a purpose.

Our text concludes: "lest ye be wearied and faint in your minds." So many times we faint and grow weary. We don't seem to have the energy to keep going. We are too tired to read, pray, and meditate upon the Word of God. Instead of running, we walk, crawl, or worse yet, stop moving toward God altogether.

Do you feel weary and fainthearted now? Remember, God knows your every circumstance. He knows all about your weariness and weakness from the contradiction of sinners against you. He will not condemn you, but neither does He want you to remain in that condition. He says, "Consider him that endured such contradiction of sinners against himself, lest ye be wearied and faint in your minds" (v. 3). *"Consider Him!"*—that's what you are called to do. If you would endure in the race, consider Jesus' endurance in the race. Jesus is the best antidote for weariness and fainting while you are running the Christian race.

When you are afflicted, look to Jesus. Study the prophecies about Him, but especially the gospels and the epistles that most fully reveal His example and teaching. Consider how He endured affliction, and you will learn from Him how to endure as well.

Are you contemplating Christ as you seek to endure in the Christian race? If not, you will faint and will be overtaken by sin. You will fall and repeatedly backslide as long as you will not consider Him. Pray for grace to look to Christ on a daily basis in every area of your life as you battle against hindrances and sin and strive for righteousness.

Dear young people, it can be so tempting to give up your fight against sin. "I'll just give in once," you say, "because all my friends are committing this sin, and I don't want to be different. I don't want to come across as too holy." In the end, you lose the energy to say no to sin one more time, to stand up one more time for what is right and good. But dear friends, consider Christ; He did not give in even once. He walked the road to Golgotha without hesitancy. Look to Him, so that you might walk as He walked.

And when you do fall, as fall you shall, time and time again, fly to Christ. Fly to Him a thousand times. Do not try to hide from God. Once when my son was a small boy, I was going to punish him severely for a serious moral infraction. But before I could do that, he ran to me as soon as he saw me, hugged me, and with tears dripping down my neck, pleaded for my forgiveness. That is how we should run to God.

As parents, office-bearers, or employees, we often feel like we are going to faint. We are weary and preoccupied with obligations in every sphere of life. We don't seem to have time or take time to be holy. Our prayers and Bible readings are pitifully short and shallow. *"Consider Him"*—the great office-bearer who endured the cross. Let your energy and endurance derive from Him.

Do not put your heart in this world. This world

will soon end. As Spurgeon said, "If you had got all the world you would have got nothing after your coffin lid was shut but grave dust in your mouth."

Dear friends, look to Jesus now; look to Him to persevere in seeking Him. If you say, "Lord, I have prayed so long and been to church so many times, and I am still not saved, so I will stop using the means of grace"—you will go from bad to worse. Stop trying to persevere in your own strength. Look to Jesus for perseverance and endurance. Remember, He endured the cross to save sinners such as you and me. He now invites you to come to Him just as you are. If you do not come to Him, you are despising His endurance and His shame—and do you dare to do *that?* Keep pleading the Word of God; Jesus is faithful and will fulfill His own Word.

We are called to look every day to Jesus, the author and finisher of faith. So consider Him, refocus on Him, cling to Him. Meditate upon His suffering and upon His victory as the Son of God at the Father's right hand. Let His grace strengthen you from day to day. Inspired by the example of Christ and encouraged by the accomplishment of the saints, your weariness will be banished and your faintness of mind will be dispelled. In their place, your faith, courage, and strength will be renewed, and by grace, you will walk as He walked.

Oh, to be able to say with Paul as the time of our departure draws near: "I have fought a good fight, I have finished my course, I have kept the faith; henceforth there is laid up for me a crown of righteousness, which the Lord, the righteous judge, shall give me at that day: and not to me only, but unto all them also that love his appearing" (2 Tim. 4:7-8). Then, on the last day, you will meet Him as He is, and He will say, "Well done, thou good and faithful servant…enter thou into the joy of thy lord" (Matt. 25:21). You've endured the race, looking to Jesus.

Jesus will then be all in all in the sin-free land of Beulah. There will be no more sin, no more temptation, no more tears or pain or cross-bearing, but only glory in Emmanuel's land. You will forever walk as the Lord Jesus walks, enjoying Him, basking in His smile, bathing in His love, feasting in His presence. Your soul and body will be absolutely perfect. Jesus Christ will delight in you as His perfect bride, and you will be able to say to Him, "Finally Lord, I am what I always wanted to be from the moment I was born again, for now I can serve Thee with a perfect eye, a perfect body, and a perfect soul."

When former President Gerald Ford was buried in his hometown of Grand Rapids last week, the newspapers were filled with pictures of some of the tens of thousands of people that lined the streets and paid their last respects. The most common sign they displayed said simply, "Welcome home!" That, dear believer, is what your Savior will one day say to you. "Welcome home. Welcome to the eternal joy set before you—the joy of walking perfectly as Jesus walked, eternity without end."

I close with a prayer of John Calvin: "Grant, almighty God, that as Thou art graciously pleased daily to set before us Thy certain and sure will, we may open our eyes and ears and raise all our thoughts to that which not only reveals to us what is right, but also confirms us in a sound mind, so that we may go on in the race of true religion and never turn aside, whatever Satan and his demons may devise against us; but that we may stand firm and persevere, until, having finished our warfare, we shall at length come unto that blessed rest which has been prepared for us in heaven by Jesus Christ our Lord. Amen."

Study Guide

Study #1: **Jesus' Crossbearing and Ours**

1. Think of some ways in which we are to walk as Jesus Christ did. Should we *always* walk as He walked and do what He did? Why or why not? Support your answer with concrete examples.

2. How is crossbearing, as Calvin said, "an intimate part of the Christian life"?

3. How is your faith currently being tested through crossbearing?

4. Why did Jesus have to become a "cursed outcast" to finish His work?

5. Why did Simon of Cyrene initially have to be compelled to carry the cross?

6. Have you ever felt that you were "in the wrong place at the wrong time," resulting in an affliction of some sort? How did God use that to teach you that you were "in the right place at the right time"?

7. What weighed most heavily on Christ as He bore Calvary's cross?

8. Why do we resist crossbearing so strenuously when we know that all things work together for good to those that love God (Rom. 8:28)? How can this be overcome?

9. What encouragement can we glean from realizing that Simon of Cyrene was the father of Rufus?

10. How is your identity linked with a crucified Jesus?

11. Explain how God's chastening is inseparable from His love.

12. Why should Christians refrain from pitying themselves when they are called to bear crosses?

13. List and meditate on ten Christ-centered motives and purposes that God has for asking us to bear our crosses behind Jesus. Can you think of additional motives and purposes?

14. How can we tell if we are carrying *Christ-given* crosses or *self-imposed* crosses?

Study #2: **Jesus' Office Bearing and Ours**

1. Why can't your spouse or anyone else meet all your needs?

2. In what ways does Jesus warn us today to beware of sin?

3. How does Satan "bait his hook according to our appetites"?

4. Why did Peter brush aside Jesus' prophetic warning? Do we all too often ignore God's warnings to us today? If so, why?

5. How does Satan sift us as wheat? How does Christ overrule that sifting? Provide an example from your own life.

6. What do we learn when we are in Satan's sieve?

7. Satan and Jesus both want you. Contrast their desires. Who has the better claim to have us? Why?

8. Why does Jesus only pray that Simon Peter's *faith* won't fail? Why doesn't Christ deliver us today from all the sieves of Satan?

9. What does Christ's perpetual intercession at the Father's right hand mean for you?

10. Explain how the word *when* in the concluding words of Luke 22:31-32—"*when* thou art converted"—reveals the kingly office of Jesus Christ.

11. What is repentance? How does it differ from faith? Can it ever be separated from faith? Explain your answer from Scripture.

12. How should we who are believers strengthen our brothers and sisters in the faith today? List three specific ways in which you could improve in this area and ask God to give you grace to do so.

13. How could we better reflect Christ's prophetical office as prophets for Him in our homes, at school, at work, and in society?

14. How could we better reflect Christ's priestly office as priests for Him in our homes, at school, at work, and in society?

15. How could we better reflect Christ's kingly office as kings for Him in our homes, at school, at work, and in society?

Study #3: Jesus' Tears and Ours

1. How do Jesus' tears prove His humanity?

2. Define Jesus' compassion. Can He have compassion on us when we sin? Why or why not?

3. When Christ wept at Bethany, He "groaned in the spirit." Why were His tears at Bethany primarily tears of *groaning* rather than tears of *sympathy?*

4. In what ways should Jesus' resurrection of Lazarus encourage us, and how should it admonish us?

5. What steps can we take in our lives to stop taking all of God's rich blessings and opportunities for granted?

6. Why should we take God's warnings much more seriously than we are prone to do? How does our culture around us—even the Christian culture—downplay the doctrines of judgment and damnation?

7. How should we respond to God's invitations? How should His invitations humble us?

8. Provide examples of special times of *divine visitation*.

9. What does it mean to have our tears put in "God's bottle" (Ps. 56:8) and to shed tears "not to be repented of" (2 Cor. 7:10)? Are these tears sinless? What do you weep over in relation to sin and sinners?

10. If we truly viewed every unconverted person as a mission field, how would that change the way we talk and relate to them?

11. What do Jesus' tears of agony in Gethsemane teach us about our sins and our salvation?

12. How can our tears be motivated by (1) godly fear, (2) divine love, and (3) redemption's price?

13. Consider the story of the Scottish Highland shepherd boy who was instrumental in saving the lives of many people. How is this a fit comparison to Jesus Christ's sacrifice for sinners such as you and I? Where does the comparison break down—that is, how was that boy not like Christ?

Study #4: **Jesus' Endurance and Ours**

1. Why is it easy to begin something in the Christian life and in church, but so much harder to persevere in it?

2. Why were the Christian Jews in the book of Hebrews tempted to stop running the Christian race? How does Satan tempt us today to abandon the faith?

3. How is the Christian life much like a marathon race?

4. Why is it critical to rid ourselves of sin and hindrances in running the Christian race? What means can you use to help you do that?

5. Why does a Christian have no business sinning?

6. Explain the importance of running the Christian race by looking to Jesus.

7. What is the most astonishing truth about Christ "enduring the cross"? How should what Christ endured encourage us as we run the Christian race?

8. How does considering Jesus' crosses affect the way we view our own?

9. How should we be encouraged in running the Christian race by what Jesus rejoiced in ("the joy that was set before him," Heb. 12:2) and by what He despised ("despising the shame," Heb. 12:2)?

10. What can we learn from the saints in ages past and those who surround us today to encourage us to persevere in running the Christian race?

11. Why is it so important for us not only to read and study the Scriptures and the histories of biblical saints, but also to study the lives and read the writings of godly forefathers who have run the race before us (cf. Heb. 11)?

12. How does Christ's endurance equip you with strength and peace of mind?

13. How can you "consider him," i.e., Christ (Heb. 12:3), more frequently and consistently as you face life's daily challenges in running the Christian race?

14. How can we balance out our duties for this life with our homesickness for heaven?

Scripture Index

Also available from
Reformation Heritage Books

MEET THE PURITANS
Joel R. Beeke and Randall J. Pederson
978-1-60178-000-3   Hardback, 935 pages

Meet the Puritans provides a biographical and theological introduction to the Puritans whose works have been reprinted in the last fifty years, and also gives helpful summaries and insightful analyses of those reprinted works. It contains nearly 150 biographical entries, and nearly 700 summaries of reprinted works.

Bryntirion Press

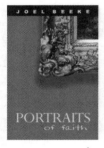

PORTRAITS OF FAITH
Joel R. Beeke
1-85049-202-6   Paperback, 104 pages

This book investigates four aspects of saving faith as they operate in the lives of particular biblical characters. Learn about childlike faith from Adam and Eve, submissive faith from the Shunammite woman, mature faith from the Canaanite woman, and persevering faith from Caleb.

STRIVING AGAINST SATAN
Joel R. Beeke
1-85049-219-0   Paperback, 126 pages

Here is a sober, practical perspective on the Christian's great adversary. It examines the personality and history of Satan, exploits his weaknesses, exposes his strategies, and encourages resolve in believers to stand firm and defeat Satan in Christian faith.